ONLY MOAN IF YOU'RE MAKING LOVE…

Only Moan if You're Making Love...

LESSONS FROM LIFE, OUR GREATEST TEACHER

IAN LYNCH

Copyright © 2025 by Ian Lynch

The right of Ian Lynch to be identified as the Author of this Work has been asserted to him in accordance with copyright law.

ISBN: 9798275180893

DEDICATION

This book is dedicated to people who choose to dedicate their lives to the service of others and the betterment of our world.

About the Author

Ian Lynch is writer, speaker, coach and guide. He has featured as a happiness expert on the BBC, Channel 5 and various radio programmes and was a former member of Robert Holden's Happiness Project and Success Intelligence. He is an advocate for creating inner peace in an ever-changing and noisier world. He is available for speaking engagements, media articles and for one-to-one sessions. You can find out more about his latest work and contact him via *www.ianlynch.net*.

Also by the author: *Rites of Man* (ISBN 978-1-9993529-8-1) prepared for publication by Drombeg Books, West Cork, Ireland. © Ian Lynch 2020

ACKNOWLEDGMENTS

I would like to acknowledge and thank the following people whose support and friendship were inspirational in enabling me to write this book.

To Tom O'Driscoll, for badgering me in the best of ways to turn an idea and some musings into this book. There is no doubt in my mind that if it wasn't for you Tom, *Only Moan If You're Making Love* would still be just an idea.

To my sisters, Celia and Julia for your love and support during the highs and lows of my life. Thank you for believing in me and loving me through thick and thin, with the exception, perhaps, of my time as a driving instructor and '*Hawkwind*' fan.

To Robert Holden, for giving me the opportunity to work with you for seven years and be a part of The Happiness Project and Success Intelligence. We had a ton of fun and our brotherhood is one that I value deeply and enjoy immensely.

To Robert Norton, for your support, friendship and musical genius over twenty-five years. Thank you for creating some beautiful meditations with me. I always enjoy our moments together and I look forward to the next time.

To Russ Hudson, for your dedication to teaching and sharing the wisdom of The Enneagram and for your friendship and wise counsel. I always cherish my time in your company.

To Val, for having known me since 1975 and not judged or criticized me once. Thank you for being there in my darkest moments, and for sharing some really good times over the years.

To Dave and Sean for being such great moral support and a source of one or two of the stories and priceless moments that appear in this book. Thank you both for welcoming me into your shire.

To Mike, Nick and Paul for your friendship and encouragement, and of course, the many laughs and life lessons that we have shared over the years. Long may they continue.

To Akushi, for teaching me so much about generosity and letting things go. We flew high in our bi-plane and had some fun times doing so. May you continue to fly high along your path.

To Sally Mudge, for your support and encouragement in helping me to get going with the writing of the first couple of chapters of 'Only Moan', and for our many conversations over chocolate and wine about love, unity and crop circles. Thank you so much.

To Jane Ferguson, for laughing at my book title and demonstrating that it also works to quieten down unnecessary moaning.

To Wendy, for believing in my writing and nudging me towards becoming a better man. I am eternally grateful. Good luck on your adventures, you will always have a place in my heart.

To Con Hurley. Thank you as always for your friendship and sage advice. Our business meetings are always the best.

To Andy Thomas, for inviting me to speak at The Glastonbury Symposium, and giving me the opportunity to come out of my shadow and back into the light.

To Ayse Turk, for pushing me into booking a launch date for this book, thus giving me a deadline to work to, and for goading me into giving a talk and singing in public.

To Jon and Rachid, we had some fun as the three amigos, and it was great to have your support when this book was far away from being a reality.

To Gloria Urech, for your inspirational artwork and design. I recommend anyone who is looking for quality bespoke artwork to check out her work at www.gukuukistudio.com. Thank you. I look forward to our next collaboration.

To Maurice Sweeney of Menma Books (www.menmabooks.eu) for your help and assistance in publishing this book. I am grateful to you as always, for your wisdom and guidance.

To all my friends, partners and those who have crossed my path, alive and in spirit, who I have not been able to mention personally. Thank you. You have all put a smile on my face in your various ways.

And finally, to those who resonate with point seven on The Enneagram, especially those who have a sexual, social and self-preservation instinctual stack, and a six wing. We know that we are not really 'a seven'. We are far too enthusiastic and playful to be just one thing. Let's keep shining our universal light. The world needs the depth of joy that we carry in our hearts and souls more than ever. Let us carry on partying with life into the wee hours, and then again tomorrow, forever.

CONTENTS

Acknowledgments	vii
Introduction	1
Prologue: How it all Began	3
Chapter 1: Only Moan if You're Making Love	21
Chapter 2: Stack the Odds in Your Favour	35
Chapter 3: Here to Help	51
Chapter 4: Keep Growing Until the End	65
Chapter 5: Sometimes, You've Just Got to Laugh	79
Chapter 6: And the Opposite of Life is..?	97
Chapter 7: Setting Sail for The Shores of the Heart	113
Epilogue: A New Chapter Begins	125
Notes and References	*131*

INTRODUCTION

Only Moan If You're Making Love is a memoir of 'life lessons' that contains moments of comedy, pearls of wisdom and times of sadness and grief, when staying alive became success. From all of these experiences, together with the many years I have spent reading, learning, watching and facilitating sessions and workshops on happiness, success and love, with all the obstacles that can get in their way, I have distilled seven important lessons that make our lives easier, sweeter and more rewarding.

As Mark Twain purportedly observed; "Good decisions come from experience. Experience comes from making bad decisions." *Only Moan If You're Making Love* is an account of some of the decisions that I have made, good and bad, and the wisdom that I gleaned from them. One of my aims is to illustrate how difficult situations can, with time, turn out to be badly wrapped gifts that lead to transformation for the better. On the other hand, a once perceived 'good' thing can turn rotten, just like rancid fruit. The old adage of 'good, bad, who can say?' is worth remembering and applying as is necessary.

I hope that each chapter will get you to think about your own life, as by taking stock of the beliefs and actions that have led you to where you are today, you can evaluate what has worked and what has not, and take the best course of action in future.

When I was twenty-one, I was aboard a ferry heading towards the port of Dover. I was travelling with three friends as we returned home from a four-week inter-rail trip around Europe. One of them, Dave, pointed at the famous white cliffs rising in the distance and asked me' "do you think you could swim to shore from here?" I replied that I probably couldn't. He then asked me; "but what if you had to?", to which I replied, "well in that case I probably could." The reasons behind why we do or do not do things is worth our investigation, for the quality of our lives depends upon our attitude and our decision-making. Whether we stagnate or evolve rests in our hands.

If I had to choose one particular lesson to offer you up front, then it would be to never let the 'old man or old woman' take a hold of your zest for life with its thirst for knowledge and desire for growth. Keep open to the spirit of adventure and don't let fear or judgment stop you from expanding your horizons and going after all that your heart yearns for. Despite its craziness, and our craziness to match, our short and precious lives are worth giving everything we have to making the most of them. May you inspire others with your wisdom and uniqueness, and may you be blessed with a fruitful, fun and fulfilling life.

Ian Lynch, November 2025

PROLOGUE:
HOW IT ALL BEGAN

ARRIVAL

I was thrust into the world in 1960, fifteen billion years after time and space exploded into being, before transforming itself over the millennia into the leafy streets and avenues of Harpenden, a small commuter town just north of London. I was born at The Red House, one of numerous cottage-style hospitals dotted all over the country prior to the creation of the industrial sized complexes that we see today. Back then, I just thought of myself as Ian, a boy who loved to play and smile at the wonder of it all. I had much to learn about the miracle of existence and the human take on it, so for now, it was a teddy bear, milk teeth and a few toys in a playpen to keep me amused as I slowly began to get to grips with the way of things.

SWEATERS AND BLANKETS

The nineteen-sixties were part of an era of knitted sweaters given as presents or gifts for birthdays and Christmas, with mum's, aunties, grannies and next-door neighbours all chipping in with an item or two. Green, red, yellow, blue and white, with beige for the older folk, seemed to be the most popular, with the odd multi-coloured patterned one to jazz things up. Whilst a newly knitted sweater was kind of exciting at first, within a year or so, all woollen sweaters seemed to expand around the waist to become baggy and uncool. Some of them were doomed from the moment that the first stitch had been cast. Due to a rationing mentality that lingered from the war, sweaters were often passed down from older sibling or cousin. We were told not to worry about their oversize-fit, for we would soon grow into them. This proved to be a lie, for as we grew, so did the sweaters. When Mrs Brown, our next-door neighbour, left for the great knitting room in the sky, the last of these hand-crafted garments was gone. Mass production was taking their place.

As scratchy, uncomfortable and uncool as knitted sweaters could be, they were a required item of clothing, for the winters of the nineteen-sixties were cold enough to form icicles on the inside of our windows. There was as yet no central heating with only two log and coal fires to huddle around; one in the kitchen and one in the lounge. Winter flannelette sheets, a hot water bottle, an eiderdown, two or three blankets and thick cotton stripy pyjamas were all necessary to help prevent us from being cryogenically frozen overnight. If we were good, a tiny fan heater provided pre-bedtime respite from the chill that permeated the upstairs rooms of our house. There was, however, one small silver-lining to the incessant cold of these early childhood years. After a night-time visit from 'Jack Frost', I would pick off the icicles that formed on the inside of my bedroom windows and suck them, as if they were an ice lolly treat handed out on a hot summer's day.

I soon learned that the brown ones were to be avoided for they tasted metallic and gritty, similar to the taste that could be found by licking the ice that formed on the door frames of my parents Austin Cambridge estate car.

Learning by trial and error was the way of things back then, and as the folks of the day used to say; 'a little bit of dirt doesn't hurt', which was basically true unless the dirt happened to be dog-poo. This had the annoying habit of hiding under fallen leaves or disguising itself as small stones that looked perfect for small boys to throw into a pond. Health and safety in those days was a good whack around the ear or a telling off if you ripped your clothes or ran off too far. Using common sense was deemed good enough for most other situations. Boys of course will be boys, so skinned knees, black eyes, bandaged heads and trips to the Accident & Emergency Department were part of growing up.

LET IT SNOW

Outside the house, there was a winter wonderland waiting to be explored. Heavy snowfalls were perfect for tobogganing, snow ball fights, toffee apples and tomato soup. We had a fantastic local common, with secret places to play hide and seek in an area known as the 'ups and downs'. There was also a pond and a sandpit, and an overgrown and abandoned horse racing course that added to the fun. In town, we had a Victorian-styled public park called Rothamsted, which had a long avenue of lime trees, swings and slides, half a dozen football pitches and a deep dell that was used for sledging. The town itself was like a small oasis surrounded by countryside. For those who love to spend time in nature, as I do, it was a blessing to grow up in such a wonderful setting.

There was magic in the air during those cold winter days. The cool, crisp breeze mixed with the smoke from coal and log fires that billowed up into the sky from the chimney pots of almost every home. This created a sense and feeling of community with everyone bracing themselves against the elements. It was homely, inviting and somewhat Dickensian. Little did I know that it was becoming an end of an era.

1973 saw the first of a series of coal-miner's strikes in the U.K. that brought electricity power cuts, candle lit evenings and a three-day working week. For us schoolkids, it meant three days of school and two extra days of bonus holiday time. Over the following couple of decades, coal production and usage started to decline, central heating became the norm, and winters in the south of England turned milder.

THE TIMES, THEY WERE A CHANGING

The sixties were a decade of great transformation in my life. From reading children's books, I soon progressed to reading comics such as The Beezer, The Beano and Lion and Eagle. The Beano introduced me to 'knock down ginger', the art of ringing someone's door bell and running off before they opened it. The Lion and Eagle taught me how to bring down a 'Doddle Bug' flying bomb, if I happened to run out of ammunition in my Spitfire plane, or save myself from a herd of charging buffalo should I only have one bullet left in my rifle. This was invaluable information for a seven-year-old boy. We used our imagination to make wild camps in the woods and play cowboys and Indians, save the world from 'the little green men from Mars', and climb trees, which sometimes ended in tears, cuts and broken bones. We were muddy, resourceful and care free.

Inside the house, my mum and aunt, Auntie Mavis, talked excitedly about the new third television channel, BBC 2,[1] whilst our twin tub washing machine, spun and shook the whole kitchen with its spin cycle. An attachable hose took the soapy waste water out through an opened side door and into the drain. This whole process was utterly fascinating and it was a sad day when an 'all in one' device entered our house and washing clothes became fully automated and dull.

Auntie Mavis was a godsend, she was fashionable and funny and she introduced me to a 'pop group' who were taking the charts by storm, called 'The Beatles'. Their song *'She Loves You'*[2] was at number one in the charts. The Beatles were to provide the soundtrack to my formative years, ably supported by 'The Monkees'[3], with their zaniness and fun-loving antics.

In 1967, I officially joined *'The Summer of Love'*,[4] in spirit at least, by deciding to try a delicious looking shiny berry called 'Belladonna'[5], which sounded edible, only to be told that it also had another name, 'Deadly Nightshade'. As I didn't fall to the floor immediately, I didn't think too much more about it, until I started to feel sick, threw up and went into a feverish semi-coma that brought on hallucinations. The worst of these was when I saw grotesque goblins coming out of the walls and down from the ceiling, making hideous groaning sounds as they looked at me with devilish intent. After several house-calls and treatments from both Doctor Hester and Doctor Bird, I was finally given the all clear. As the years passed, I began to wonder if I had imagined those experiences, until one day in my early forties, I lay in bed feeling groggy and nauseous after drinking 'magic mushroom' tea, and hey presto, the same goblin guys were back and 'pissed', groaning and moaning as grotesquely as they had done before.

Around the time of my first psychoactive trip, something important happened in our family. A younger sister arrived, almost out of nowhere it seemed, to be ceremonially plonked down onto the kitchen table in a carry cot, for Celia and me to gape at. Our family of four became five, as Julia joined the house of fun. This turned me into a middle child with all the responsibility and challenge that this position brings.

As Julia grew into a young woman, I decided that for her seventeenth birthday the perfect gift would be to teach her to drive. I chose the local swimming pool and tennis club car park on an early Sunday morning in October, knowing that both sports would be closed for the season. This would give us plenty of space to make a start. The lesson lasted all of three minutes. With just one other car parked in the far corner, Julia set off straight for it with the acceleration of a Formula 1 racing driver. I pulled on the handbrake and shouted: "Stop". In the same moment, I got to realise why real driving instructors have duel controls. Three things then happened. Firstly, I retired as a driving instructor with immediate effect. Secondly, I apologised to Julia profusely, and thirdly, I paid for her to have a professional lesson a week later. My baby sister in the cot was now gearing up to fly the nest. Time was racing by.

MUSIC, MY THIRD LOVE
After my aunt brought the 'Fab Four' and their songs to my attention, music began to rival my first two loves of football and spending time in nature. Simon and Garfunkel, T.Rex, The Who, Hawkwind, Bob Dylan and others began to enrich my world. We sang *'Yellow Submarine'* [6] on a school trip, bashed out *'Sugar Sugar'* [7] in the playground and I started to take an interest in the charts. A music festival called Woodstock [8] became front page news, as hundreds of thousands of people revelled in the mud and the sunshine in some far away field. They were 'drop-outs' according to my father. According to my grandmother and aunt, long haired men could now be mistaken for women,

whilst at school, my elder sister was told off for showing too much leg below her skirt. My mum, aunt and Celia wore Chelsea boots, and I started to grow my dark brown curly hair longer and longer to look like Marc Bolan[9].

THE CHIMES OF BIG BEN

It was a sad day when the nineteen-sixties came to an end. The Mercury, Gemini and Apollo missions[10], Star Trek[11], England winning the World Cup at football and the rise and demise of The Beatles were now confined to a previous decade. The nineteen-seventies seemed dull and boring when they first arrived, and it took me until 1972 to adjust and start to enjoy them and the music they spawned. No end of a decade has ever touched me as strongly or as deeply as the passing of the sixties. It will be odd and amusing if I live long enough to see 'the sixties' return, that is of course, if I remember the first lot, which as some of you may know, means that I wasn't really there.

TIME TO LEARN SOME LESSONS

Back in 1968, my parents decided that my wild and excitable ways needed a stronger form or educational guidance, and so I was taken out of state junior school and sent to a private establishment called 'Moreton End Preparatory School for Boys'. Unlike the modern, newly built school that I had become used to, this was an old, slightly scary looking Victorian building, which had a basement cellar that led to the partially blocked entrance of a second-world war air-raid shelter, housed under the main lawn.

Soon after I joined the school, I learnt what the Headmaster called 'a lesson', which was a cuff around the head for being cheeky or not paying attention. Corporal punishment was part and parcel of schooling and it didn't take me long to realise that it was also a badge of honour amongst the pupils at Moreton End to be hit. The harder and more numerous the canings, slipperings or blows to the head, the more kudos a pupil would attain, especially if the trigger for the belt was a witty response to one of the teachers, and so, I began to cut my teeth as one of the class clowns. I also had a lot of catching up to do, for the standard of education at Moreton End was higher than I had been used to at my previous school, The Grove. There, 'Stig of the Dump'[12] had been considered advanced literature. Here, we were being tutored for the public schools of England.

I despised being made to do anything and had absolutely hated being forced by my parents to learn the 'times-table' off by heart. Being hit by the Headmaster and told off for not spelling onomatopoeia correctly at the age of eight made me all the more determined to rebel against such ruthless autocracy, as well as get up to speed as quickly as I could. There were many days when Moreton End was an absolute hellhole and I would stand solemnly in the playground during lunchbreaks, like a Steve McQueen character in *Papillon* or *The Great Escape*[13], and stare forlornly out of the gates at the cars and the people who passed me by. They were free to go about their lives as they wished and I longed to join them.

WHEN DREAMS COME TRUE

Ironically, one of the most aggressive teachers, Mr Thompson, taught geography, a subject that I fell in love with immediately. I chose to learn the capital of every single county in the world, including Ouagadougou, the capital of Upper Volta. That was until the country changed its name to Burkina Faso in 1984, and I started to lose this knowledge. Back in the days of Mr Thompson, I used to make up imaginary tropical islands at home, drawing and colouring them onto sheets of blank paper, before pretending to swim in their warm and inviting waters. I lived the dream in my bamboo hut, made from blankets and a clothes horse.

Many years later, on a round the world adventure, I visited One Foot Island, (Tapuaetai)[14], a small exotic atoll of The Cook Islands, where I got to swim in the warm waters of this idyllic haven, and walk on its golden beaches, just as 'Robinson Crusoe'[15] might have done. It felt as if I had somehow been transported through time and space into one of my own imaginary creations. Mr Thompson had sparked my interest, nature and adventure had called to me, a friend called June had said go to The Cook Islands, and suddenly there I was, swimming in my own childhood drawing.

When the day came to say goodbye to Moreton End,

Mr Thompson spoke with my mother about his career being ruined during the war, which had resulted in him ending up in Harpenden at this small private establishment. This explained a lot. He wished me well, turned and suddenly, it was over. I stepped out of the school gate for the last time and joined the free world. Pastures new were beckoning me on.

Today, I have great compassion for Mr Thompson, for like most, if not all of us, he was born into this world with high hopes of leading a happy life, only for circumstances beyond his control to take him in another direction. Instead of university, he had headed off to war. As John Lennon sang so poignantly in his song *Beautiful Boy*[16]; 'life is what happens to you when you're busy making other plans'.

SCHOOLS OUT FOREVER

When I arrived at Roundwood Park in the autumn of 1971, I was ahead of most of my classmates on the school curriculum. I cruised into the first set of every streamed subject, without having to learn much at all. I entered my class speaking contest and won. The prize was to talk in a competition in front of the whole school. For such a challenge, I was not prepared or tutored. As I began my speech, a teacher who was sat right at the front, who I'll refer to as Mr B, made a joke at my expense causing everyone to laugh. I fell apart and was voted out. It was an embarrassing humiliation.

Years later, I joined an organisation called *'Toastmasters'*[17] and began to learn the art of public speaking with confidence. As I progressed to become a professional speaker, I imagined going back in time to that exact moment of my ill-fated school speech contest. I let the laughter die down before asking Mr B to stand up in front of everyone. I then 'roasted' him brutally, demonstrating that what the schools of the future needed most, was far better and more encouraging teachers. Although it gave me great pleasure to rewrite history, and I might even have won the contest, I would not choose to change a thing. I have learnt that victories and failures are equal opportunities for learning and growth, although I definitely prefer the former to the latter.

In my second year at secondary school, a new love showed up in my life, girls. Going to a mixed school was proving to be way more fun than the boys only one that I had been to previously. I was introduced to a wonderful new world of touch and intimacy, which brought new feelings and very pleasant sensations to enjoy. We played spin the bottle for kisses in our breaks, started partying and drinking on the weekend, and shared our puberty years fumbling about as we grew to understand the art of sex. Making love was yet to come. One of our teachers, Mr Clayton, gave us a worthy life lesson. He told us that any boy or man who was worth his salt would always ensure that he got his girlfriend home safely. I took this to heart and then one step further when I walked an older drunken man home from the pub late at night, to protect him from potential harm from some unruly guys on the street. Girls led to dancing and listening to other styles of music. Donna Summer arrived on the scene, Barry White crooned and sang about love, and handbags joined us on the dance floors of the local pubs and clubs that we were now frequenting.

With each passing year, we gained more knowledge and more freedom. This went up a notch noticeably, during our final year of schooling as some of us began to drive. One lunchtime, for the eighteenth birthday of one of our mates, Gav, we decided to head off to The Three Horseshoes, a pub on Harpenden Common that had taken its name from the town's horse racing past. We celebrated with a few beers and a game or two of darts. By the time we left, Gav was 'three sheets to the wind' and the rest of us a little merry and boisterous. One of our two drivers, who we shall call C, the eldest boy in our year, decided that overtaking the first car out of the carpark, would be a fun and entertaining thing to do. Accelerating with a wheel spin of his mother's Datsun Cherry, he drove across someone's freshly mowed front lawn and cut inside, forcing the other driver, Nick, in a beautiful red and shiny Austin 1300, to swerve to avoid a collision or a head on crash into a fast approaching telegraph pole. To this day, I do not know how we all survived unscathed and with neither car damaged, which alas, was more than could be said about the now rutted front lawn.

The final exams came and we headed off into the big wide world to make our way. As Alice Cooper had sung to us a few years earlier, 'schools were out forever' [18]. The University of Life had opened its doors.

THE ROAD TO HAPPINESS AND SELF-KNOWLEDGE

Before I went on to further studies in higher education or had started working fulltime, I went on a two-week vacation with the venture scouts to Switzerland in order to climb and hike in the mountains. It was a biannual pilgrimage. One hot and lazy afternoon, I decided to walk up the slopes and sit down by myself to contemplate life. It was my first attempt at meditating and shifting my consciousness. I lay on my back, fascinated with the peaks that rose up into the sky on the other side of the Rhone Valley, up above the bustling town of Sion. It seemed incredible how small we humans were compared to the snow-capped summits and alpine pastures that were in front of me. The sound of cow-bells added a Buddhist like zen quality to the whole experience and I began to find myself seeing inside the mountain. Jewelled caverns and crystal caves dazzled in equal beauty to the magnificence that I was observing on the outside. Time seemed to slow down and then flash by.

When my stomach began to rumble, I decided to get up and head back down to where we were staying, as it was fast approaching dinner time. To say that my legs were burnt to a crisp is an understatement. I was like a red boiled lobster, and had to waddle slowly down the mountainside in agony. Over dinner, my thighs became a target for a playful slap or two, and the beauty of the moment on the hillside started to fade with the setting sun. However, if I choose to remember that extraordinary afternoon, I can return to that slope in my minds-eye in an instant, enter again that cool mountain interior, and not have to worry about sun burn.

SALES AND SELF-DEVELOPMENT

After I left school, I went into business with Jeff, a friend from school, setting up an aquatic shop at a local garden centre and installing a variety of fish tanks, vivarium's and ponds in people's homes and work places. I decided to make a career in sales, eventually becoming a partner in an office equipment company. I also continued to study, gaining a psychology and social science Hons degree through The Open University [19], as well as completing a variety of courses and trainings in restorative justice, therapeutic practices and coaching. I became fascinated with self-development, and the thoughts and attitudes that can make us happy or throw us off the cliffs of despair into the depths of depression. I read books, listened to tapes and CD's, watched videos and went to lots and lots of workshops. The opportunity came to work with Dr Robert Holden at Success Intelligence and The Happiness Project, which I took, and began a seven-year voyage that was to change my life. I dived on in, learned to run courses, workshops and events, became a happiness expert on television, radio and in the media, and coached and helped others with their lives. It was a beautiful and expansive time and a perfect coming together of desire, passion and destiny.

A LEAP INTO THE FIRE TO RISE AGAIN

After seven years exploring happiness, success and love, I grew a little restless and allowed the impulsiveness of my head to take a hold of my heart. A new opportunity arose to be involved in a social media start up called Woby (The Wold Birthday Connection), based around the twenty odd million people who share the same birthday every single day across the planet. I decided to leave Success Intelligence and take a chance on taking this venture to market. Although it had great potential in so many ways, it was not to be. The business ran out of investment capital before it could be successfully launched and I, like others, lost a substantial amount of money. It was a tough and painful time.

Soon after, my parents became ill and died. I went travelling, wrote my first book, *'Rites of Man'* [20] and lived a life of riley without realising that I was losing my moorings and my direction. When finally, the consequences of my wild excesses came home to roost, I crashed down badly and fell apart. Hope for a happy future faded and I very nearly gave up on life, so desperately sad had I become.

Thankfully, with the love of my sisters and support from

close friends, I began to pick myself up and take a good look at my life. I began to laugh once again, as I remembered some of the amazing things that I had done, seen and experienced. I started to journal and reflect on some of the lessons that I had learnt, forgotten about and was now revisiting with humility, and the kind of wisdom that can only be gained from having such a fall from grace. I took some temporary work and dug in, remembering a wonderful line from the book, *Tuesdays with Morrie*[21] by Mitch Albom, when Morrie, who had been diagnosed with Lou Gehrig's disease, said to himself: "Do I wither up and disappear, or do I make the best of my time left?" I didn't want to let my life wither away, so I committed to making the best of the years I had left, however long or short that would prove to be.

Eventually, as my smile and self-belief returned, this book began to 'write itself', almost as if it had a mind of its own. When the last chapter arrived, one message was loud and clear. Whenever an ending arrives, a new beginning commences, even though we may not see it or feel it at first. Life, in part, is definitely what we choose to make of it, and I hope very much that you will make the most of every chapter in your own life, by living wisely, wildly and majestically. May you stay young at heart and timeless in spirit.

CHAPTER 1:

ONLY MOAN IF YOU'RE MAKING LOVE

A TITLE AND A SAYING IN THE MAKING

When I was working with a driving agency, I travelled to Loughborough in Leicestershire to collect a van that was to be delivered to North Wales. I arrived at the large depot and gave the site controller the registration plate details. After a minute or two, I was told that there was a problem: The vehicle I was after couldn't be found anywhere on their system. This was not that uncommon in this type of work, so I could easily have moaned and 'gone off on one' had I chosen to. Instead I smiled and stood to one side to let the next person have their turn. As I waited patiently for an update, a supervisor at the depot, called Jane, told me that she was planning to write a book about her life and some of the funny things that had happened to her. Jane felt she could provide some useful life lessons to share with others. As we chatted about her ideas, I told her that ironically, I had just started to write a book about life lessons myself. Jane asked me what the title of my book was, and when I told her, she burst out laughing and said that she would be using my expression herself. As if by design, one of her colleagues came around the corner wearing a long face and began to complain about all and sundry including my missing van. Quick as a flash Jane blurted out: "Oi, only moan if you're having sex." The guy stopped in his tracks, we laughed, he moaned and then muttered something before heading off. Perhaps I was birthing a new saying as much as a new book.

Three weeks later, after a beautiful sunny country walk in the Chiltern Hills, I was having lunch with some friends when one of the group, who knew of my book title, said out loud; "so Ian, do you moan?" I looked at her with mock stunned expression, ignored the temptation to say; "invite me round for dinner and let's find out" and simply said, "I beg your pardon?" Everyone laughed, for that was not what she had meant. The truth was that I had been guilty of moaning and being grumpy more times than I would care to admit, and that, in part, was the reason behind the title of this book.

MOANING AND COMPLAINING
Life presents many situations that will challenge, test and stretch us, and yet we will probably create just as many, if not more, ourselves. Some of the most difficult problems we face will only ever exist in the wild imagination of our fertile minds. Another quote attributed to Mark Twain says amusingly: "I've lived through some terrible things in my life, some of which actually happened." Whether or not he actually said this, the sentiment remains true. Learning to master our subconscious thoughts and beliefs is perhaps the most difficult task we face as a human being. I am sure that if life gave us everything we wanted, when we wanted it, there would still be plenty of people

who would find fault with something, and then start to moan and complain about it.

Over the course of our lives it will undoubtedly be necessary to complain in order to get things changed or corrected. If we are up against it, it is only natural to feel stressed and less accommodating of others. Once the challenge has been tackled, letting go of such feelings and frustrations is much better than creating a story of suffering to tell everyone we meet. After all, we all have our own upsets and ordeals. That's life. Moaning about the same old things over and over again, whilst doing nothing in particular to change them, is not only deadly dull but a killer of energy and a waste of precious life time.

Serial moaners are a vexation to the spirit, and who in their right mind wants to be like that or be around someone who is? Rather than being bitter about life, it's much smarter to try and make things better and remember that we do have a choice in the attitude we take. Brian Tracy, one of the most prominent experts and guides in helping to make people's lives better, says in his book *Flight Plan*[1]: "If you are a positive and constructive person, you accept a high degree of responsibility for yourself and for everything that happens to you. You do not blame other people or make excuses. If you are not happy with a situation, you get busy and do something to change it. And if you can't change it, you accept it. But you never complain."

Even just a slight moan or a minor complaint can make all the difference between enjoying a happy and fulfilling day or creating one of upset and drudgery. It is wise to put things into perspective and count to ten, or even eleven, before opening our mouths. As Richard Carlson championed in his book *Don't Sweat the Small Stuff*[2]; 'Argue for your limitations and they're yours.' If we allow the little things in life to swallow us up, we will be far less likely to enjoy moaning for pleasure.

A GOOD REASON TO MOAN

I took a trip to Esalen with a new girlfriend to attend a writing workshop led by Mark Matousek[3] and enjoy the beauty and tranquillity of this magical place. If you have not been, 'The Esalen Institute'[4] plays host to a retreat and learning centre that is situated on the Californian coast just off of the Pacific Highway near Big Sur. This is a stunning and much filmed coastal drive that has featured in many a Hollywood movie. Esalen itself is a magnificent setting with hot tubs, amazing views of the ocean, lush gardens and a fabulous swimming pool to boot. Due to a mix up and our late arrival, someone had taken our place in our allocated dormitory and was actually asleep in one of our sleeping bags, laid out before we had unloaded the rest of our car. Homeless for the night, as the office was now closed, I built us a love nest next to the swimming pool. The night was warm and inviting, and with the pool all to ourselves under a star-studded sky, we did the only sensible thing that young lovers could do, and went skinny dipping. We were in love and in lust, so we made love in the water, in our love nest, and again in the morning to welcome in the sunrise. As there was no one about, as far as we could see, I allowed myself to moan at full volume. As our passion subsided and we held each other tightly, noises started to come from below, and to our surprise, a woman who had possibly been meditating in the garden next to the pool, stood up and headed towards the dining area for breakfast. If we didn't already have a smile on our faces, we certainly did now. It appeared that we had all been saying 'Oh God' in our own heavenly ways.

As our relationship grew, so did my moaning in other areas of my life. I was off track and out of balance, having put myself under financial pressure to complete my first book, *Rites of Man*[5], and I had become somewhat overly-sensitive and snappy. Whilst making love al fresco can be sexy and romantic, providing of course there are no mosquitos or ants to join the party, complaining and being niggly certainly isn't. Sadly, but with little surprise in hindsight, my girlfriend left me and I lost a lover, a dear friend and a soul mate. The moral was not lost on me: Moaning for the right reasons is great but for the wrong ones, it is a repellent. The lesson was tough. I collapsed, broke down, got back up and the title of this book was born.

WHINGING, HAKAS AND HUGS

Whenever I go on a long road journey, I enjoy listening to music and often use my travels as an opportunity to catch up on something new or listen to a few blasts from the past. As I was singing along to *Lazy Sunday*[6] by The Small Faces, a conversational lyric in the song reminded me of the fun and games that we British can sometimes have over complaining and not complaining. This is particularly noticeable amongst the post Second World War generation. When asked; 'Hello, how are you?' some of the most common responses include 'bearing up', 'soldiering on' and 'mustn't grumble', the one used in the song. Whilst maintaining a stiff upper lip and trying hard not to cause a fuss by complaining unnecessarily, the Brits were coined 'The Whinging Poms'[7] by some Australians, for the amount of moaning and whinging that they did when they ventured down under. We can complain about small and insignificant things, particularly the weather, and yet we can also put up with unacceptable situations for way too long by trying to be polite so as not to cause a fuss. Ironically, and perhaps because of this paradox, Brits are often at their best when the chips are down. This seems to bring forth a gallows sense of humour where we laugh at ourselves and pretty much everyone and everything else. Spike Milligan, Monty Python, Sean Lock, Billy Connolly and many others, have brilliantly created jokes and sketches that show the madness of our tribulations. Brits are masters of understatement, after all, as The Black Night[8] says in Monty Python and The Holy Grail: "It's only a flesh wound."

Several years ago, my partner Sally and I took a holiday

to Australia and New Zealand. After having fun travelling up and down the East Coast of Australia, we headed off to Auckland to visit my Kiwi cousins Ros and Jill and spend time with my uncle, Ross, on the beautiful Coromandel Peninsula. As part of our trip, we wanted to experience some Maori culture up close and visit the hot volcanic springs at Rotorua. Sally saw that there was an opportunity to take part in a 'Hangi'[9], a traditional feast using heated rocks to build an oven. It would also feature dancing and other traditional festivities, and so we signed up.

When the day arrived, we took a taxi to the organisers offices where five coaches were waiting to take all guests to the feast. We were met with a long delay and no forthcoming information as to what was going on and when we might actually be setting off. As many of the tourists and guests seemed unwilling to question this, possibly because they were British, I decided to ask one of the Maori guides, who had just appeared. I politely asked; "Excuse me, could you give us an update on what is happening and when we might expect to be leaving?" His response was short and muffled as he angrily brushed me off with a scowl and turned toward one of the coaches. I looked around at the many people lined up waiting behind me, many of whom were naturally interested in what this guy had to say. I turned back towards him, gestured towards the other guests and in my loudest voice said: "Excuse me, we've paid good money for this experience and we'd all like to know what the hell is going on." He stopped in his tracks with a look of thunder on his face at my calling him out. He was a big guy but he weighed up the situation as everyone was now watching and said; "I will go and find out."

When he returned, he told us that we could begin boarding the buses and so Sally and I got onto his coach, and sat right at the front, directly opposite the driver's seat. Once we were all on board, our miserable and grumpy guide morphed into 'Mr Jolly' and he began to explain the proceedings and what we could expect across the evening. He explained that there would be an opportunity for one person to do the 'Hongi'[10], the sacred Maori greeting of pressing noses together, which I had seen done on television with Heads of State whenever they visited New Zealand. To choose which person to take up the Maori Challenge, it would require one volunteer from each of the five coaches. Then the Warrior Chief would decide which of these 'Volunteer Chiefs' would become 'Chief of Chiefs' and take up the Challenge. Our driver friend asked who would like to be the chief of our coach, and my arm shot up into the air immediately. The driver looked at me with his familiar scowl, and asked if there was anyone else who might be interested? I turned around to look at the other passengers with my arm still in the air and no one moved an inch. Reluctantly, the driver took me as our chief.

As we dismounted from the buses, the five chiefs were ushered over to form a line facing the Wharenui[11], a traditional communal house. As everyone watched, the Warrior Chief came out of the building with a weapon held above his head. Having got this far, I had determined that I was going to be the one to take up the challenge and so I faced the warrior, clenched my fists by my side, and did not take my eyes off of his for a second. The Chief laid down 'The Challenge' onto the ground and took two paces backwards in ceremonial style with his tongue sticking out threateningly and his weapon at the ready. As I kept my eyes trained on his, I suddenly felt a sharp slap on my shoulder from my nemesis the coach driver. I was indeed to be the chosen one. I stepped forward and with eyes still firmly on the Maori Warrior Chief, walked up to him, bent down without lowering my gaze, and took up The Challenge. We then performed this ancient and noble greeting. It was an honour and a privilege and it made up for the earlier shenanigans.

The feast began and I settled down with Sally to dine and watch the entertainment. Then, just as I was comfortably relaxed and enjoying my dessert, it was announced that the five 'Chiefs of the Coaches' were required to go up on stage and perform a Haka[12], a Maori ceremonial dance, made famous by 'The All Blacks' New Zealand rugby team. My head and heart dropped for I knew exactly what was about to happen. Five men were going to be as lambs to the slaughter for everyone's enjoyment and entertainment. As soon as we began, with all of the 'Coach Chiefs' trying desperately to follow the fast moves, with our tongues sticking out and various grunts and roars to be made, the laughter began in earnest. At the back of the hall, the bus driver was wetting himself, for it was pure comedy gold.

He only had eyes on one chief though, and that chief was me. It was sweet comeuppance for him. As soon as we had finished, to a hearty round of applause and some shouts for more, I walked down the steps of the stage and straight to the back of the hall, where our Maori friend was sat with his arms crossed, and a huge grin upon his face. I smiled and said; "I bet you enjoyed that." He replied that it had been wonderful and I laughed, put out my hand and said; "I'm Ian, can I buy you a drink?" He shook my hand vice like, and in a restorative moment of unity, we became like best mates chatting away about all and sundry. After the feast was over and we returned to the offices, the hug that my new friend gave me was like that from a bear, both as recompense for my complaint and for the restorative bond that we had shared as a result. Complaining and apologies in the right circumstances are much needed and sometimes, as happened to me in New Zealand, what follows can be priceless.

MAKING A STAND FOR INJUSTICE
Gandhi showed the world how the power of non-violent violent protests can change history. Peace activists from all over the world put their lives on the line to try and thwart some of the worst atrocities of human behaviour. Learning to find our voice and go against a violent or

biased narrative takes guts and resilience. One of my alltime heroes is Kathrine Switzer[13], the first woman to run the Boston Marathon in 1967 during an era of misogyny and patriarchal prejudice.

All Kathrine had wanted to do was to run and she was very good at it. In fact, she was so good that her running coach reluctantly agreed to back her application as 'K.V. Switzer' to get past the male only qualification rules so she could enter the race. Together, with her boyfriend and a few other open-minded male runners, she began the race, only to be dragged off the course by an angry race official in a violent and aggressive manner once her gender had been rumbled. Her boyfriend and one or two other runners jumped to intervene and Kathrine was able to complete the race, only to be disqualified at the finish line.

At first Kathrine was shocked and shaken by the turn of events. This soon turned to anger and a steely determination to do something about the injustice and some of the false beliefs, such as women who run long distances will harm themselves irreprovably. Thus, a woman who had simply wanted to run became a sporting activist and a campaigner for equal status.

In 1984, at the Los Angeles Olympics, the very first women's marathon was staged and Kathrine's endeavours were rewarded and honoured. Beautifully, she got to run the Boston Marathon again and this time to a rapturous reception from start to finish. In another act of redemption and reconciliation, Kathrine and the angered race official,

Jock Semple, became friends after he changed his mind about women and fell on his sword. Making a stand and complaining for a good cause had won the day.

SUPER GOOD AND GETTING BETTER

When I grew up in the nineteen-sixties the term 'Moaning Minnie' was frequently used by disgruntled parents to try to stop a child from complaining about a 'long journey' to the coast. The comedy troupe Monty Python featured a 'Complaints Department' in one of their memorable sketches *Argument Clinic,* and serial moaners were often written into the soap operas of the day as 'pantomime' villains.

An expression 'SNIOP' was created by the motivational speaker Zig Ziglar[14] to describe someone who had become 'susceptible to the negative influence of others', most notably the moaners, complainers and cynics. The advice Ziglar gave to deal with moaners was to get to know who you are, master your own attitude and change the channel whenever you could. I used to love to practice this last idea, namely that if someone was on a negative offensive and asked me how I felt, I would respond with Zig's channel changing phrase of 'super good and getting better'. When I worked in sales, one hilarious colleague from Liverpool would climb onto his desk and go 'whoop-whoop yes-yes' if ever the conversation in the office began to turn moany. It was brilliant to watch. Anything that successfully interrupts a negative pattern can help us to snap out of our malaise. Comedy and silliness are especially useful for raising disheartened spirits, interrupting patterns, and waking us up.

CHEERS AND MOANS

I heard a wonderful anecdote from the sports journalist Jim White about the late great Ray Clemence, one of the best goalkeepers to ever grace a football pitch. The team he played for at the time, Liverpool, had just lost the 1977 F.A. Cup Final, the oldest major sporting tournament in the world, to their arch rivals Manchester United. Distraught and annoyed with themselves, the players lined up at Watford Junction railway station, for the long trophy-less journey back home to Liverpool. They were crestfallen and quiet, when Clemence suddenly walked to the edge of the platform and with his suit jacket over his shoulder, turned, and began to dance. He twisted and moved like Jagger to the applause of his teammates who clapped in rhythm. When he finally twirled to a finish, he said something like; "Cheer up you lot, we've got the European Cup Final on Wednesday and we're not going to lose that game, are we?" [15] The sour mood lifted and Liverpool went on to create football history, winning the final. Just as Ray Clemence got his team mates to shift their attitude from one of doom and gloom to belief and determination, we can all shift our body language and our mood in an instant, once we know how and remember to do it. We can learn to praise rather than criticise, we can put things into perspective and we can look towards the future, rather than down at what is past and gone. If you choose to look on the bright side of life more often than you do the negative, you will sing and dance with life like Ray did, a lot more frequently.

As you and I are for the most part in charge of our thoughts and our voices, we can speak up whenever it is appropriate and necessary to do so, and ignore trivial matters rather than waste our precious time and energy upon them. Shit and shift happen. The Serenity prayer, written by Reinhold Niebuhr in the 1930's, invites us to accept the things that we cannot change, have the courage to change the things that we can, and have the wisdom to know the difference. Then we can save our moans for tough, painful and worthwhile challenges, hitting a winning tennis shot, pretending to be a ghost, or having sex and making love.

LIFE LESSONS # 1

Φ Don't sweat the small stuff. Put things into perspective and save your moaning for the big and worthwhile occasions.

Φ If you can change a situation for the better, then be the change, and change it.

Φ Look for opportunities to heal rifts. Forgiveness and reconciliation take away reasons to moan.

Φ Make love not war. Be a lover not a fighter. If you find yourself sweating on the small stuff, then it just might be time to get yourself laid.

CHAPTER 2:
STACK THE ODDS IN YOUR FAVOUR

WHAT ARE THE ODDS?

In the late 1990's, I qualified for a business trip to Las Vegas. This was an incentive reward set by the Swiss manufacturer FRAMA AG for sales people and directors of U.K. based office equipment companies who achieved their yearly targets. As we gathered at Heathrow Airport for the start of our 'jolly', Steve, a fellow director, decided to buy a book for the flight on how to win at the casino and swat-up on strategies and tips for winning at craps. Mercifully, I have never been interested in gambling, with only the odd alcoholically induced bet for fun or bravado, to my name. I listened half-heartedly as Steve talked about which numbers were best to bet on, when to pass or not pass a line, but most importantly, to walk away whenever you went up on your stake money. Most of this went in one ear and out of the other. I started to glaze over, chose a movie, and sat back to relax and enjoy the rest of the flight.

Once in Vegas, FRAMA AG laid on a fabulous experience including a spectacular flight over the Grand Canyon, jet skiing near the Hoover Dam, tickets to see the singer Tom Jones, lavish meals and of course, a trip to the casino. We were staying at The Luxor, an Egyptian themed resort hotel which had its own night club. I was thus able to wish the gamblers good luck for their evening and head upstairs to have some proper fun and dance the night away.

When I finally left the club, I saw Steve standing at a craps table with a couple of the others, and so I decided to head on over and see what it was all about. With a complimentary drink in my hand, I watched them play, trying to remember some of the things that I had heard on the plane.

Sure enough, when Steve went up on his stake, he walked away and took a break. At the end of our five-day excursion, Steve had won $1200 on the craps tables. Whilst gambling is a not something I would recommend to anyone, by doing his research and putting the tips that he had read into practice, Steve had definitely stacked the odds in his favour.

A MISSED OPPORTUNITY

On occasion, I have only realised what success was after I have lost something, whether that be a relationship, a work position or an opportunity I didn't take. One such moment occurred when I was lying in bed on a Sunday morning, listening to the radio and cuddling up with my girlfriend. After the obligatory news bulletin, a competition was announced to win two tickets to see the group *Bananarama*[1] perform in Singapore, and get to meet them afterwards. All you had to do was correctly give the maiden name of the singer Siobhan, who at the time was married to Dave Stewart from *The Eurythmics*. I thought that most people would know the answer, and so I stayed put, as the DJ began playing the band's song *'Robert De Niro's Waiting'*.

The first caller to give an answer was miles off, as was the second, the third, the fourth and the fifth, at which point, I looked at my girlfriend, jumped out of bed and grabbed the phone. I dialled the number as quickly as I could on the good old-fashioned landline, and just as it started to ring, caller number six guessed correctly. I slammed the phone down as Steve Wright's character '*Mr Angry*' might have done, and ruefully climbed back into bed. Had I acted immediately and got through, then my girlfriend and I could well have been heading off to Singapore rather than St. Albans market. Instead, I was left to reflect on all the times that I had spent working with Siobhan and her sister Moira, at our local supermarket and chatting together as we walked home from our respective schools.

Had I known a maxim of anthropologist Thomas Huxley[3]; "Do what you should do, when you should do it, whether you feel like it or not", then I would have reached for the phone before the first caller had time to answer incorrectly. Wayne Gretsky, an all-time ice-hockey great observed sagely: "You miss every shot you don't take." If another opportunity ever arises on a relaxing Sunday morning lay in, I won't hesitate, I'll be like Wayne and 'take the shot'.

PLANNING FOR A GOOD LIFE

When I first became interested in 'self-development', I gorged myself on books, courses and good old-fashioned inspirational tapes. I listened endlessly to the likes of Brian Tracy and Tony Robbins, and the wonderfully entertaining motivational speaker from Texas, Zig Ziglar. His slow southern drawl and anecdotal story-telling were infectious, with none better than the one he told about Howard Hill. I loved this story so much that I used to be able to recall it almost exactly word for word as Zig did, so here goes.

"Now the name Howard Hill might mean something to some of you and nothing to the rest of you. Howard Hill was known as the greatest archer who ever lived. He entered one-hundred and ninety-six tournaments and placed first, one-hundred and ninety-six times. I've seen him take an arrow and shoot it straight into the centre of a target some three hundred feet away and then take a second arrow, and split the first one completely in two. Now, I'm an archery expert, par excellence, which means I'm really good in French. In fact, I'm so good that I could teach each and every one of you, providing your eyesight and your health were normal, to shoot better than Howard Hill could on the very best day of his life . . . providing of course, that we first blind-folded Howard Hill and then spun him around until he had no idea where the target was. Now, you might say; "That's ridiculous Ziglar, how can anyone hit a target that they can't even see?" Well I've got a better question for you. How can you hit a target that you don't even have? If you want to succeed in life, you've got to have goals and take the necessary steps to achieve them."

Brian Tracy, a giant in the field of success and self-development, says, "If you fail to plan you plan to fail". Once you have a plan, as Tony Robbins hammers home: "You've got to take MASSIVE action."

WHAT IS SUCCESS?

For seven years I had a dream job working with Dr Robert Holden[4], and team, at Success Intelligence and The Happiness Project. We worked on three of the most important aspects of our lives: Love, happiness and success. One of my most rewarding tasks was to organise and manage our public events, where we explored these topics experientially in workshop settings. I was privileged to witness some breathtakingly beautiful breakthroughs and powerful insights shared by many delegates, participating in some of the exercises whenever I could.

One of my favourites was a three-day programme simply called 'Success Intelligence'. We limited this event to a small select group of sixty people from our client and public databases for maximum personal interaction. As we gathered at the hotel for coffees and teas before the course began, one gentleman stood out to me in particular. He was tall and immaculately dressed in a sharp pin striped suit. It was no surprise to find out that he worked in the City of London financial district. Once the event had got into full swing, we broke into small groups for conversational exercises on success, both in our work places and our private lives. At the end of an amazing first day, there was overnight homework to undertake; go home and have a conversation on what success means for our partners, family or a close friend.

Day two started with a recap and an open space for questions and feedback on day one. I noticed that the man who had been so well suited and booted was now dressed in smart casual. He was one of the first to speak and share how the opening day and the homework had impacted upon him. Firstly, it had dawned on him that if he didn't make good on a promise to take his daughter to school, instead of leaving early each morning for his office, then it would soon be too late, for she was well into her secondary education. Secondly, when he had asked his children what success and happiness meant to them, his son had responded by saying; "going to the park to fly our kites like we used to do".

Both had shocked and surprised him. By stopping to think about real success, it had shown him just how much his life had become overly centred around his work, climbing the old career ladder, and that as a result, he was missing out on precious time with his family, time that he would never be able to get back. On the final day of the workshop, he arrived dressed for the beach in cut-off jeans and a t-shirt. The simple act of taking time-out to define success through deep and honest conversation had changed his outlook and his demeanour. His transformation and candour sill touches me to this very day.

If you have never had a conversation on success, happiness or love with your family or a loved one, I strongly recommend that you do. It might be one of the best and most important conversations that you will ever have and it all begins by defining it for yourself.

SUCCESS OVER TIME
Of all the events that I have facilitated personally, one of the most profound was a one-day happiness and success workshop held in Rome for owners and senior executives within the chain making industry. This was everything from tiny mechanisms found inside a watch, to the largest sea anchors in the world. It was fascinating to meet such a diverse group of business people together with their partners.

I had decided to incorporate a wonderful exercise that I loved from our *Success Intelligence* course, and so to demonstrate how it worked, I needed a volunteer to come out to the front. A happy and jolly gentleman from France raised his hand, stood up to a round of applause, and came forward to join me. Laid out on the floor were a series of seven laminated sheets with 5, 15, 25, 5 years ago, Now, 5 years-time and 85 printed onto them. I invited the man to step onto the first sheet and asked him what success had been for him at age five? His response surprised me at first, for he said milk. Then I got it. He described a post-second world war France, where drinking milk had become a luxury as the country recovered from the fighting and destruction, which necessitated the rationing of precious food items. At age fifteen, success was ... "aving sex", for after all, as he said; "I am French".

As we progressed through each of the ages and a success for each one, we finally arrived at the last sheet, eighty-five, which represented the wisdom of our Eldership years. I asked him to step onto the sheet and turn around to look back at the one that said 'Now'.

I then posed my question: "If there was one piece of advice that you could give to yourself, right now, from standing here at age eighty-five, what would it be?" With a deep intake of breath, and a tear in his eye, he said: "Spend more time with my beautiful wife". As he turned to look at his wife with both hands on his heart, we all went 'awww'.

When we get down to the nitty gritty of what's truly important in our lives, success often shows up with tears of joy and hugs of gratitude. This workshop moment proved to be no exception.

GETTING TO KNOW OURSELVES
I first came across the Enneagram when I was invited to attend an event in London facilitated by renowned authors and teachers, Don Richard Riso and Russ Hudson[5]. I didn't have enough time to read up on this great body of work before the course started, so I quickly scanned the nine

key points outlined on the back of their seminal book *An Introduction to the Enneagram.* As soon as I reached point number seven, *The Enthusiast*, I knew instantly that this was 'my type.' I did a short version of their RHETI test, and it confirmed my initial prognosis. As we began, I sat back, happy to be identified as a fun-loving enthusiast. Don and Russ began by looking at point eight out of the nine, leaving point seven for the last session on the last day.

I had been feeling pretty smug as I listened to the virtues, desires and wake-up calls for each of the points that Don and Russ took us through, until finally, it was time to examine point seven. It did not take long before my heart began to sink, I crossed my arms and started to squirm uncomfortably in my seat. It was as if someone had been stalking me my whole life, compiling a detailed report on every moment of spontaneity, every prank and every all-night party that I had ever gone to. Worse, they had written a specially extended section on my fears, sadness and chronic worries about missing out on love and the life that I was meant to be living. It was galling to see how robotic and predictable my behaviour was, and have it revealed so publicly. Charlie, a fellow number seven, shared in my pain and sorrow. We were brothers in arms as our hidden tragedy was so brutally exposed.

Thankfully, it did not have to be this way, as Don and Russ so gratefully revealed. There are red flags in the behaviour patterns of all nine points that we can learn to spot, stop, and see that we have a choice to respond differently. There are practices to help us manage our instincts and excesses and become the person that we truly want to be; the person who in essence, we already were. Understanding why we act out in the ways that we do, particularly under stress, is of paramount importance if we wish to stack the odds in our favour, fulfil our potential and live happier, wiser and richer lives.

Together with other deep investigative self-inquiry bodies of work, 'The Enneagram' is like a psychological and spiritual guide; one that can lead us to the best of our unique and truest nature. It is why NLP (Neuro-Linguistic Programming) and psycho-somatic therapies such as EFT (Emotional Freedom Technique) and Havening, are so useful in helping to overcome self-limiting and harmful thoughts that have become stuck in our bodies and minds. Our personality is not the same as our essence or soul. Instead it is a series of responses and beliefs that we developed mostly during our childhood into subconscious and predictable patterns of behaviour.

I was enthralled with all that Don and Russ had to share, as I was with all of the other transformational modalities that I came across. As any 'good' boy who has developed a point seven type personality might have done, I dived on in, and started to study and practice them all.

QUIETENING A CHATTERING MIND
Having a creative mind is a blessing and a curse. Whilst it is great to have lots of cool ideas to get to work on, it

is another matter entirely to lay awake night after night plagued with a mind chattering away like a troop of monkeys. Sleeping with a note-book by the side of the bed can help, but it can also give permission for more of the same. Learning and practicing meditation, which initially seemed like a complete waste of time when I was frazzled and busy, has proved to be a life-saver. St. Francis de Sales, an open-minded former Catholic Bishop of Geneva, is quoted as saying: "Half an hour's meditation each day is essential, except when you are busy. Then a full hour is needed."

In 2018, I had the perfect opportunity to put this into practice in some style: One hour of meditation, before dawn, in the King's Chamber of The Great Pyramid at Giza. Together with other lucky explorers who had travelled with Russ Hudson and John Alexander West[6], we were invited to find a suitable place to prepare ourselves. Then, the lights were turned out. I shut my eyes and eagerly began to meditate, hoping for a divine or cosmic experience, which might change my life. Within moments, I was thinking about a cat that I'd had as a boy, how uncomfortable I was sitting on the floor, the incredible breakfast that I would be eating in a couple of hours, and whether or not the people who had built the pyramids were extra-terrestrials. Whilst the room was quieter than a library, my mind was as loud as a noisy marketplace. I gave up, let go of my expectations, and finally my mind began to settle.

Hitting the off switch in our minds is an art that requires practice and commitment. Our incredible biological processor needs some help from ourselves to slow down and relax. Only then can we experience a deeper consciousness to the usual bunch of conflicting and bewildering thoughts. Such moments can prove to be like the USS Enterprise[7] going into warp speed. A whole new way of experiencing ourselves, and life, materialises as the everyday chatter begins to dematerialise. Everything changes, everything expands, and we can see the world and our choices from a calmer and wiser perspective. Sometimes it's been possible to have an experience of 'leaving my body' and experiencing 'the blue' as I call it; a place of utter bliss with nothing except an azure light all around me. Mostly Its simply a feeling of being that doesn't need to speak in English. We are not our thoughts or even our bodies, although we are very much reliant upon them.

BEING PREPARED FOR THE UNEXPECTED

The motto of the Scout movement, 'Be Prepared', coined by its founder Lord Robert Baden-Powell[8], was a cornerstone of my days in the movement, no more so than when we were preparing to go hiking or camping. In these cases, 'Be Prepared' meant packing a space blanket, an orange rain coat, a Swiss army knife and a bar of Kendal Mint-Cake into an already overflowing rucksack. On one particular trip to Scotland, this meticulous planning went to the dogs.

A trip had been arranged to take a ferry from mainland

Scotland to the Isle of Arran and climb its highest peak, Goat Fell, and then afterwards, camp in a field before returning to our base near Loch Lomond on the following day. When the time came to get ready, four of us were informed that we would have to make do with a cobbled together dining shelter arrangement. After we reluctantly but dutifully accepted, we set off somewhat annoyed at what had happened, but nevertheless determined to make it work. By the time we arrived at the start of our hike, the weather could hardly have been worse, with torrential rain and high winds. Undeterred, and with gritted teeth, we set off for the summit.

After attaining our goal, we headed as quickly as we could to the camp site. Instead of a grassy field with some shelter from the wind, we were met with a marshy bog, which would have made the mud of Glastonbury or Woodstock seem like a croquet lawn. As we unpacked the dining shelter, it soon became evident that we had been given the wrong poles to set it up properly. Three of us decided to give up and take our chances back in town, with one determined character called Owen, refusing to give in. We left him to it and set off to try to reach the town before sunset. When we approached the port of Brodick, we found a beach hut with a broken door, and took some much-welcomed shelter from the storm. Shivering in our soaking wet hiking gear, we changed into dry clothes, thankfully packed and prepared inside waterproof bags, and tried to get some sleep.

As the sun began to rise, we were met with two unexpected sights: A Royal Naval vessel anchored in the bay and clear blue skies. Rejoicing at this unexpected good fortune, we stripped off into shorts, laid out our wet clothing in the sunshine, and went for a swim to freshen up. Then, we went off to find some breakfast. By the time the others had arrived, ragged and bedraggled, we had eaten heartily and were in good spirits playing football on the beach with our clothing dry and neatly packed away into our rucksacks. Owen was not annoyed in the slightest, though he was desperate for a cigarette, for his packet had disintegrated into mush before he had even had the chance of a single puff. We laughed, gave him a cigarette and everyone got into the sunshine groove. As the saying goes, if something can go wrong it usually will. Being prepared means being ready to expect the unexpected.

OUR ATTITUDE AND RESPONSES ARE IN OUR OWN HANDS

Unless we are physically or psychologically afflicted in any way, we are either master or servant to our attitude and responses. The responsibility buck stops firmly with each one of us. We can study and learn how our personality works and find out where and how we can make some adjustments. We can practice patience, resilience and putting things into perspective. "Success", as Winston Churchill liked to say, "consists of going from failure to failure without any loss of enthusiasm." If we slip up, we can recommit to doing better next time. We can be kind to ourselves and to others, although at times, this can be easier said than done. When that happens, we can remember to be kind once again.

We can regularly check in on our relationship with money, where we might be undervaluing ourselves and our income, or making money more important than our loved ones, our health or the natural world, and if we choose to, we can say 'yes to the best and no to the rest'.

If we really want to stack the life odds more firmly in our favour, we have to keep growing, be adaptive and stay alert to the opportunities that come our way.

LIFE LESSONS # 2

Φ Know what success truly is for you and your loved ones. Then go after it with everything you have.

Φ Don't hesitate. Take the shot. Better to miss by a mile than miss out altogether.

Φ Get to know what makes you tick. Then tick rather than tock. Don't let your personality get in the way of your true nature.

Φ Turn off your mind so you can think more clearly. Take time out to tune in.

Φ Be prepared. Poor preparat ion leads to piss poor performance.

CHAPTER 3:
HERE TO HELP

A GOLDEN PATH TO HAPPINESS

One of the fastest and most enjoyable ways to create meaning, purpose and happiness is to be found by helping others and doing our best to make our world a better place. The principle of 'do to others whatever you would have them do to you' is a foundation of all healthy human relationships.

Being of help and support to others is also a wonderful healer for the spirit. The more time and attention that we give to making a difference in other people's lives, the more our own troubles seem to shrink by proportion. As we move from focussing on 'only me', to focussing on 'me and we together', our heart can open wider with compassion and joy, making it much harder to become grumpy or lonely.

THE SECRET OF WINNING TEAMS

The most successful teams in all walks of life are primarily those that create a strong and devoted team spirit where everybody looks out for one another, plays to each other's strengths, and covers for any slips or weaknesses, should they happen to occur. Such teams foster a camaraderie that becomes rock solid, especially when the team comes under pressure. It makes a huge difference to know that someone has got your back. Johan Cruyff[1], one of the greatest players and coaches to ever grace a soccer football pitch said: "It's like everything in football and life. You need to look, you need to think, you need to move, you need to find space, you need to help others. It's very simple in the end".

The 'improv comedy' teacher and leadership coach John Cremer[2] reminds his audiences and his students alike that improvisational comedy works at its best when each player helps the others to develop a scene to its funniest conclusion. You go with, rather than against, whatever is said.

A Course in Miracles[3], one of the modern era's greatest books on self-awareness and inner peace explains poetically that giving and receiving are two aspects of the same cycle for in truth, they are as one. When we give and receive wholeheartedly, all parties become blessed.

HONEYMOON BLESSINGS

I went on my honeymoon vacation to the island of Corfu in Greece, where my wife and I took a day trip to Albania to visit the ancient Greco-Roman city of Butrint. Now it would be rude of me not to mention our voyage from Corfu to Albania, on what was a very choppy day, so much so that it made the small tourist boat rock from side to side and bob up and down in the swell. As it was a special holiday, we bought a couple of beers from the small cabin at the front of the boat and took them back to our seats in the stern to toast one another. It was a hot day and as we were feeling the newlywed vibe, we decided to have another couple of beers, as the first two had gone down so well. I stood up, empty bottle in each hand, and strode toward the tiny bar. Suddenly, the boat lurched to port and I was thrust towards a young woman, leant over the side, enjoying the ocean view. There was no possibility to stop myself and the empty bottle in my left hand struck her from behind about mid-ship. She took off like a rocket with the shock and surprise of this unexpected intrusion and only the quick actions of her partner prevented her from going overboard. In response to witnessing this incident, my wife nearly fell off the back of the boat herself, together with one or two others.

In fact, along with the unfortunate woman and her partner, I think I was the only other person on board who didn't seem to enjoy the spectacle of this near tragic incident. I apologised profusely, went to the bar, and with fresh beers in each hand, turned and braced myself, like a gunslinger, ready for the return journey.

With everyone watching and waiting as if it was indeed the 'O.K. Corral'[4], I said out loud, "three, two, one" and set off knowing that disaster was just another big swell away. Thankfully, my goal was attained safely and everyone onboard could once again focus on their Albanian adventure. If the expression 'comedy is tragedy plus time' holds true, then I hope that the unfortunate couple on the boat are now able to see the funny side themselves.

After we docked, it was just a short coach ride from the modern East European styled harbour, with its newly built waterfront apartments, to the ancient and magnificent ruins of Butrint. Our tour guide was a lovely woman who had a great historical knowledge and a friendly demeanour. She oozed passion and joy as she shared the secrets and beauty of this cultural delight. The views from the citadel along the river and out toward the ocean were breath-taking. Sail boats shimmered under the bright blue sky in contrast to the deep blue waters of the Mediterranean Sea.

When our tour came to an end, we were driven back to the harbour and everyone began to disembark the coach. I then had a conundrum, for the cash that I had exchanged into Albanian Lek was the equivalent of a single one-hundred-dollar bill.

Most of the other tourists seemed to be tipping either ten or twenty dollars and so I hesitated to hand over the larger note. However, my wife was insistent and so despite my slight reservation, I handed it over to our wonderful guide. She looked at it and then looked me in the eye, burst into tears and hugged me tightly. I was shocked and humbled by her gratitude, especially after my miserly deliberations. It made the day and was an utterly priceless experience. I was and always will be grateful to my wife for her wisdom and her good heart, and to our guide for her response, for I received as much, if not more, than I had given.

A LESSON DURING COVID

When I came back to the U.K. in 2020 following four-months travelling in Asia, I needed to earn some money whilst I worked out the next chapter of my life. As the impact of the global pandemic began to take effect, I saw an online advert for Government funded 'Covid-Testers' at the nearby University of Cranfield [5]. This was a technology led college with a leaning toward the aviation industry. It was also one of life's irony's, for when I had been a karate student in my mid-twenties, I signed up for a series of aircraft evacuation trials at Cranfield. Together with a fellow karate student, Brian, we were paid twenty pounds for turning up, with a further five pounds to be earned if we managed to escape the plane in the first fifty percent of each evacuation. There were four such trials scheduled for the day. As the evacuations began, it proved to be absolute bedlam with several people requiring counselling on the grass beside the plane. This was due to the ferocious nature of the clamouring to get out of the plane in time to grab the cash. For Brian and myself, it seemed like a perfect way to make a little extra money, considering we'd probably have done it for free. However, with a strong desire to be in the first fifty percent for each trial, I found myself jumping across the seats and over others in the melee to escape. With all of the extra money on offer stuffed safely into my pocket, I mulled over how differently I might react if ever I faced a real-life aircraft evacuation. I hoped it would be very different to the 'demented dwarf', as Brian had described me, leaping about the cabin, with all thoughts on grabbing the extra cash.

Covid-testing at Cranfield proved to be a very different experience. I determined from the outset to make the testing procedure as calming as I could for those who came to the Centre, many of whom were anxious and frightened. The Site Manager in charge of my shift gave me a 'Here to Help' badged baseball cap, which I was happy to don.

Soon after we opened for 'business', I enrolled on a 'first aid at work' course to refresh my skill set in case of any medical emergencies. Less than a week after I had completed the training, one of my colleagues began to choke on a piece of chicken that he had eaten too hastily during our short lunch break. Thinking it would help, he grabbed some water and as a result was now drowning as well as choking. I reacted swiftly and gave him a sturdy whack on the back, one that some of my old school teachers would have been proud of. It didn't work, so now there was little choice other than to perform the recently practiced 'Abdominal Thrust', formerly known as the 'Heimlich-Manöver'. Thankfully, it worked superbly, and both chicken and water came flying out and one lucky man got to live to eat another day. Life had thrown up a coincidence of timing in the most literal of ways.

MY FIRST ROLE MODELS

I was blessed to have grown up in the small provincial commuter town of Harpenden, some twenty-five miles north of London. For reasons that I could never fully fathom out, Harpenden had developed a strong scouting and guiding tradition which eventually led to Harpenden Venture Scout Unit becoming one of the first in the country to become 'mixed' when we officially welcomed Ranger Guides into the fold in the autumn of 1978. A key emphasis of the scouting tradition was to learn outdoor activities for the hills, the mountains and upon the water, together with leadership skills for use in the wider world. The two leaders of the newly formed Unit were two maverick and inspirational people, Marilyn Hudson and James Kingham, QC. The difference that both of them made in people's lives over the years was massive, as anyone who knew them well will vouch for.

Sadly, James died in car crash aged sixty-nine and his memorial service, held at St. Marys Church in Luton, was packed to the rafters, such was his popularity, charm and influence. James had been a Barrister and a Circuit Judge and had championed young people throughout his career, most notably giving juvenile offenders a second chance in life by teaching them the same outdoor and leadership skills that he had taught to us.

At the service, a fellow barrister and long-term friend of James gave a magnificent eulogy recalling an incident where James had taken a group of youth offenders abseiling and rock climbing. A few weeks later, one of them had been arrested whilst abseiling down a block of flats in North London. When questioned by the Police, the young 'cat-burglar' said that it had been 'The Judge' who had taught him all he knew.

A British tabloid newspaper got hold of the story and published an article about 'lily-livered liberals' and their modern-day approach towards young offenders who should be tasked with breaking rocks and sewing up mail bags instead of gallivanting around the countryside. What this editorial failed to mention was the extraordinary success that James and others had achieved in changing the behaviour and the lives of most of these young people.

Helping others to fulfil their potential is one of the greatest accomplishments that any one of us can achieve and is definitely one of the most rewarding. Coaching and guiding others through difficulties and challenges has given me some beautiful gifts and precious moments. What would our world be like, if we were all taught to help one another and we put it into practice? The movie, *Mr Burton*[6], illustrates how one man's kindness and dedication helped nurture and transform a young wayward Welshman into becoming the actor and cinematic legend, Richard Burton.

LOOKING OUT FOR OTHERS

Many life lessons and morals have stayed with me over the years since those halcyon days with Marilyn and James. The Scout motto of *'Be Prepared'* still helps to keep me alert and on the lookout. I am born from this old school, so whenever I travel on public transport I will give up my seat to anyone who needs it more than I do.

When I was around fifty-five years old, I hopped aboard a crowded underground train in Central London to head home. As the doors shut behind me and I held onto the rail in the packed doorway, a young woman in the seat to my left stood up and said; "Would you like to sit down?" I looked at her with a bemused expression on my face as a million thoughts and responses raced through my mind. I smiled and thanked her politely, saying that I preferred to stand after sitting down for too long already. Inside, I was laughing, for how I saw and felt about myself was obviously not how this woman had seen and experienced me. I had to face up to the fact that perhaps I was no longer the young buck that I thought I still was.

Some of the best of humanity, as it can be for other species, occurs when those who are stronger protect and look out for those who are weaker. It was a sweet gesture from this younger woman and I had to accept my changing status in life with a mixture of sadness, amusement and a growing sense of eldership, with all of its possibilities, as well as its challenges.

THE GREATEST SACRIFICE

I studied for a masters in restorative justice at the University of Ulster in the city of Belfast in Northern Ireland, a fascinating place to visit and spend time in. One thing of particular interest was the Titanic Museum[7] built on the site of the Harland and Wolff shipyard where the notorious ocean liner had been completed back in 1912. No one in their right mind would have predicted a sea faring life for this 'unsinkable' ship of a little less than two weeks. As the Titanic floundered on the tragic night of April the fifteenth, there were many heroic acts, not least from those who gave up their seats in the lifeboats to women, children and the elderly.

Perhaps there is no greater glory or gift that a human being can give than by swapping or sacrificing their own life for others. What often comes to mind when I think about this, is the self-sacrifice of the site workers and rescue personnel during the two catastrophic nuclear disasters at Chernobyl and Fukushima. Ordinary folk at work suddenly became courageous souls and heroes who were determined to save as many people as they could despite knowing that their efforts would result in their own terrible demise.

    Thankfully, for most of us, there will be far less dramatic and fateful ways to be of help and service in the world around us. We can pick up some of the huge amounts of discarded litter in our towns and countryside. We can volunteer for a charitable cause, or we can simply offer kind words of assistance and support to anyone who is struggling or suffering in the face of life's challenges. There are plenty of opportunities to be a light in the world and our kindness, compassion and sense of a community spirit can make all the difference to somebody's life.

LEARNING THE ROPES

When I worked with Robert Holden at The Happiness Project, we had a wonderful exercise that we shared on some of our events that had originally been created for people who worked in the health-care profession. A long length of rope was laid out across the floor of the conference room and the delegates were asked to stand along the rope at a point from one to twenty to represent where they felt they were in terms of helping others. It was fascinating to see the dilemmas that some delegates went through in order to get to their number. Once they settled by the rope, Robert skilfully asked them a series of questions about what had brought them to that point, and what might help them to move up a number or two.

What was even more fascinating was what happened during a part two of the exercise, where the delegates were asked to stand along the length of rope once again, but this time at where they felt they were in relationship to how good they were at looking after themselves and receiving help. Most, but not all of the delegates, took a step or two backwards. The conversations that Robert struck up with the delegates was eye opening and emotive as people shared some of the reasons why there was a difference. It can be one thing to be good at helping and caring for others but a whole different ball game to ask for and receive help yourself. Thankfully, with the incredible live meditative music of Robert Norton[8], together with Robert's compassionate and inspiring words of self-appreciation and healing, the session ended in a beautiful and uplifting manner. The tears that flowed were ones of liberation and self-love, as guilt and old beliefs about receiving were washed away.

PLAYING YOUR PART

This human journey was never meant to be undertaken alone. It is not possible to be a totally self-made person, for we all need support and tools created by others to make our way. There is no doubt that people who are genuinely interested in helping other people tend to live happier, longer and more fulfilling lives than those who don't. There is no shortage of opportunities. It can be as simple as being a help rather than a hindrance in our daily interactions, or being kind, respectful and considerate, whenever possible. What better gift to give to someone than our total present awareness, for we all wish to be seen and heard for who we really are.

If our world is ever to reach a place of peace, where the last bomb and bullet have been placed safely into a museum, it will take an attitude of loving consciousness to make it happen. We all have a part to play. Unity or disunity? Love and cooperation or more fear and individualism? We can believe in separate selves or we can change the world peacefully with a 'me and we' attitude. Making peace with ourselves is a good starting point, and then together, we can then help bring more harmony and love into a world that is desperate for both.

LIFE LESSONS # 3

Φ Be to others as you would like others to be towards you. We are here to help not to get in the way of others.

Φ Giving and receiving are two sides of the same coin. As we give so shall we receive.

Φ Think we/me. Let love and unity consciousness guide your actions.

Φ As within so without. When you have peace on the inside, you can bring peace to the outside world.

CHAPTER 4:

KEEP GROWING UNTIL THE END

DON'T LET THE OLD MAN IN

One of the greatest film icons of all time, Clint Eastwood, star and director of spaghetti westerns, gun-slinging thrillers and beautiful heart touching human stories, has in my book, gifted us the greatest piece of wisdom any man or woman can take as they grow through their lives; don't let the old man or old biddy in.

Toby Keith, a fabulous country music singer, wrote the song, *'Don't Let the Old Man In'*[1] after speaking with Clint at a charity golf event. He had asked Clint the secret of his youthful exuberance and enduring film-making career. Clint's answer became the title for Toby's song, and helped to spread this piece of wisdom far and wide. If ever thoughts of 'I can't be bothered', 'it's too much trouble' or 'I'm too tired' try to convince you to be slothful, remember Clint's sage advice, hold your up high and with a smile or through gritted teeth, crack on.

Over the years, I have seen many people become old in spirit and attitude at a very young age. Thankfully, I have also seen people who stay young at heart. Some of the most inspirational are Clint Eastwood himself, Sir David Atttenborough, Tao Ponchon Lynch, Sally Mudge, Andy Elledge and Cyril Newsome, a man I worked with in my twenties. They all epitomise to me what it truly means to stay connected to our 'inner child' and to our life-force, with its desire for adventure, aliveness and beauty.

Cyril always chose to walk up the stairs to our offices, rather than ride the elevator or take the lift, a practice that I have borrowed ever since.

Sally, who is in her eighties, still dances on table tops as if the 'Summer of Love' of 1967 had never ended. She has an enthusiasm for life that is intoxicating.

Andy, who was a fellow school mate from Roundwood and a football teammate at Rothamsted and Harpenden Rovers, still plays cricket for Harpenden, albeit no longer for the first team. This last summer he hit fifty-five runs; not bad for a sixty-five-year-old who shows no signs of stopping.

Tao Porchon-Lynch was a yoga teacher, par excellence, as Zig Ziglar might say. She was also one of the most charismatic women I have ever met, with a life-story that would make a wonderful movie. I had the honour of meeting Tao when she was a mere ninety years of age, and experienced a yoga lesson from her like no other. She carried on teaching up until her death, after one hundred and one years of the most incredible and inspirational life. Tao's smile lives on in my mind as if I had just shut my eyes in front of her. RIP Tao. Thank you for your light and your charm.

Clint Eastwood was a hero from my childhood playing the 'man with no name' in Sergio Leone's masterpieces. I remember going to the cinema with four or five of my schoolmates to watch him in the movie *Where Eagles Dare*[2] (which also starred Richard Burton) and I have followed his career right up until the present day. It is fascinating to have witnessed Clint's life journey through the lens of a camera from the nineteen-sixties right up into the twenty-twenties. Whilst 'The Beatles' provided the soundtrack to my early childhood, Clint has been making movies throughout my entire life. He is relentless with an inspirational attitude that I find phenomenal.

Sir David Attenborough's documentaries about the magical kingdom of 'Mother Earth' are as beautiful today as they ever were. David's voice is timeless, and his commitment to drawing our attention to the extraordinary intricacies of nature and the plight of so many species at the hands of mankind is as stunning as it is vital. He continues to enthral and implore us in equal measure. As with Clint, Sir David has been an ever present in my life as far back as I can remember.

If ever you are challenged by a lazy, 'can't be bothered' thought, get up, dance, go for a walk, or go the extra mile: Whatever it takes. Your enjoyment of life will rise and so will your energy levels. Don't become a coach potato, instead be a legend of zest, just like Clint, Tao, David, Andy, Sally and Cyril. Keep growing until the end and keep your heart and spirit alive for as long as possible. Should you ever see me slouching or making feeble excuses for not doing something, then you have my permission to kick my ass and remind me to not let that old man in.

GETTING UP AFTER A FALL

There is an old Japanese proverb; 'fall down seven times get up eight', that encourages us to keep going, knock after knock, setback after setback, and never give up on anything that is truly important and worthwhile to us. For years I kept this saying at the back of my mind, recalling it when I either faced a difficult challenge or chose to share this maxim with others.

When I was younger, I did not have the benefit of such wisdom, but thankfully, as I grew and developed, I started to learn a variety of useful tools that I gleaned from sport, self-development books, courses, and my own life experiences. Together with adopting a spiritual outlook on life, they have helped me to navigate major challenges such as divorce, serious injury, a big career change and the demise and subsequent death of my parents. Nothing, however, prepared me for the hopelessness that I felt when my world as I knew it collapsed and everything seemed lost. All that I had learned turned to dust through a combination of neglect and a lack of focus, caused by living with little thought or concern for the future.

I could see the cliff edge of disaster approaching, but I was unable to stop myself falling down into a mental abyss of my own making. My life, I believed, was over. I told myself that I was a complete failure and that I had 'fucked everything up'. A line from the movie *Papillon*, starring Steve McQueen, taunted me: "I accuse you of the worst crime a human being can commit. I accuse you of a wasted life". There seemed no way out except to take my own life, and I began to think about driving my car off a road bridge at speed, as someone I knew, so sadly did.

At this point, a miracle arrived in the form of my sister Celia. When Celia realised just how far down the rabbit hole of despair I had fallen, she spent time reassuring and reminded me of some of the good things that life still had to offer me. Whilst I did not see or feel any of this in the slightest, I did see on her face and in her voice how frightened she was with what I might do. As I sat with her, I realised that I could not cause her or any of my family and close friends the pain and upset from taking my life. In the days that followed, this actually made me feel worse, for now I had no choice other than to carry on, still without any hope for a happy future. It was hell, as anyone who has ever been down on their knees in despair will know.

Slowly, I started to find other reasons to live for, or at the very least, distract me from my misery. I hung in there, re-read motivational works and the daily lessons from *'A Course in Miracles'*. I redoubled my efforts to connect to the realm of spirit and to the beauty of the natural world around me. Humour, socialising and music, which during my darkest days had felt like mockery from 'The Devil', slowly began to turn back into pleasure. Finally, after a year or more of digging in during my many fevered and sleepless nights, the day came when I felt happy to be alive once again. I was getting up for the eighth time and

'I cans' began to compete again with the 'I cant's' for my attention. With each positive step that I took, the clouds of despair that had been hovering over me for so long parted a little to reveal one or two glimmers of hope, and some sun rays for a brighter tomorrow. I was starting to turn the corner even though I was not yet out of the woods.

DEAR GOD OF SECOND CHANCES, HERE I AM AGAIN
When I was twenty, I travelled to Switzerland with around one hundred young men and women, boys and girls from Harpenden Venture Scouts. This was to be a two-week climbing and hiking expedition to Oberwald, a small village high in the Alps. It was my third such visit to Switzerland, having fallen in love with its mountainous terrain and lush pastures. There was also the added fun of travelling overseas with a bunch of adventurous young people of a similar age to me.

As we entered the last couple of days of our trip, myself and two friends, Jon and Nick, decided to hike and climb up to the source of the River Rhone, the Rhone Glacier. At that time of year, fast flowing water came thundering out of the glacier as a magnificent waterfall. With the hot Alpine Sun streaming down on our bare chests we set off on the mountain track towards our goal, only to find that part of the riverside path was submerged under fast flowing water and so we had to climb up to get past this obstacle.

Soon afterwards we approached a smooth steep section

of rock that fell away over a cliff face with a drop of fifty feet or so onto large boulders at the edge of the river. As I took in the magnificence of the scenery around us, I slipped on the shiny wet surface, lost my footing and began to plummet towards the edge. The slippery surface of the rock made it impossible to slow myself down and I flapped about wildly like a seal trying to catch a fish. Suddenly, a lump of rock hit my knee and I grabbed at it frantically with all my might. I was taken to full stretch and hung on for dear life. Slowly, I began to pull myself up until my chest was over the rock. I caught my breath and looked up at Jon and Nick. Jon's mouth was open wide, for he had seen me fly past him at full pelt and must have thought I was a goner. Gradually, inch by inch, I got myself back to where they were but my confidence was shot to pieces. As we headed towards some firmer ground, I had to crawl across the shiny surface on my hands, knees and feet. We decided to have lunch and sat in relative silence for a while, until I broke the ice by saying: "It's a little bit like the last supper." We laughed, but deep down, we were still in varying degrees of shock.

Once we had finished eating, we decided to crack on. We hadn't gone very far before we were met with another steep rock face to negotiate. Nick and I began to discuss how best to tackle it without ropes or pitons to aid us as we had believed this was going to be a relatively easy hike and climb. 'Be prepared' had been swapped with 'we know best'. At this point, Jon announced that he was going to head back down the way we had just come, believing it to be too dangerous to carry on. For me, that slippery slope was the last place on earth I ever wanted to see again and so Nick and I chose to push on.

After we exchanged our good lucks, Nick wedged himself against the rock face and I ran towards him and jumped up like a rugby line-out player. Nick hoisted me up and into a crack in the rockface where I positioned myself facing downwards. Then it was Nick's turn to run towards me. He jumped and I pulled him up, so that he could clamber over me and onto the ledge above. As we scrambled to reach the top of the peak we could now see in front of us the full expanse of the waterfall thundering downwards with a loud ominous roar.

When we finally reached the glacier, I spotted a sandy patch of earth in a large crevice to the left of the waterfall. It looked like the perfect spot to have a victorious photograph taken and so instinctively, I jumped down into it. When I turned around, my heart sank. There was a huge hole in the ice that I had not seen from the outside above. This led straight into the waterfall itself. When I told Nick, he laughed, and said he'd better take a photo for my parents, just in case. I had one chance to get out of this predicament alive. I would need to leap upwards and forwards from ice onto ice and hope my momentum would carry me onto the rocky ground beyond. I prayed: "Dear God of second chances, here I am again. Sorry to bother you but I could really use your help one more time."

I took some deep breaths and focused on my task with the concentration of Johnny Wilkinson, the legendary English rugby player. I took a final deep breath, leapt and dived forward. Thankfully, I caught some of the rock beyond the ice and pulled myself clear. Although somewhat humbled by dicing with death twice in two hours, I felt as alive as the fresh mountain air. The route down that we chose was a stroll by comparison to our ascent, and we could once again enjoy the beauty of this magical place.

When I remember that eventful hike today, it makes me all the more determination to never again walk down a dark path of mental negativity and remorse. In a similar vein to Private James Ryan, from the movie *Saving Private Ryan*[3], I choose to earn my second and third chances at life. As Matt Haig wrote about in his important and inspirational book, *Reasons to Stay Alive*[4], when we develop and maintain a focus on the gifts and great experiences that life can bestow, we increase our mental resilience for when life becomes challenging and tough.

THE TIME IS NIGH

There are more things to learn, to do and to see than any single life-time can allow. If we don't make a start right now, and work on something that we desire or love, then another day will have passed and there will be less opportunities than we had the day before. Time is not replaceable, though we may be lucky enough to get other chances in the future. It is best to seize the moment, and spend some time working out the life that you really want to live, and making a start on it immediately.

A wonderful book, *The Artist's Way* by Julia Cameron [5], encourages us to journal each morning, whenever possible. This enables us to download our dreams and get to see over time, patterns and ideas that we might have been too busy to notice. There is also *The Artist's Way for Retirement* with a message that it's never too late to discover some new creativity and a deeper meaning for our lives. There is no better time to make a start than today.

MAKING A SPLASH
I left it late to learn to paddle board. After thirteen knee operations, a steady and strong balance that had once earned me a karate black belt, had now turned wobbly. Nevertheless, for my sixty-second birthday, I decided to give it a whirl. Ignoring some expert advice on how best to get on the board, I hopped on and left it immediately for the bottom of the river to the amusement of all watching, especially one small boy and my tutor.

Undeterred, I had another go with the same result and this time, with even more laughter. I think the young lad thought I was doing this deliberately for his entertainment. I fell on my sword and listened to my teacher Anna. I also accepted my limitations and humbly sat on the board and took things gently and steadily as we set off along the river. A new pleasurable activity had been attempted, not mastered, but I had made a splash.

IT'S LATER THAN YOU THINK

At the wake for a wonderful man, Stan Gladwell, I met another long-time friend Tony and his wife Nette. We had much to catch up on as we not seen each other for many years. Tony had been the manager of a local football team that I had played for, before I was forced to retire early, following two major cruciate ligament injuries. We laughed just like the old times and talked about meeting up in the summer and I promised to call and arrange a time to head over to see them.

The months began to pass and soon May turned into June and then June into July. A message landed on my phone – Tony had died. I was gutted and so annoyed with myself. I sat with this for some time, grateful at least that we had met at Stan's wake and for all the happy times that we had spent together. This was a huge lesson to me. Don't put off seeing the people in your life that matter. As the song that my friend Allan Tidbury used to perform with his band, *The Ska Souls*, reminds us; *'Enjoy Yourself, It's Later Than You Think'* [6].

SWEET POETIC KARMA

When I was at Roundwood Park School, there was a wonderful lad in my year called Andy Rutherford. Andy was a man of steel. He was brilliant at sport and a true gentleman. You name it and he could do it and do it to a county level standard. If it wasn't for personal and family commitments, Andy could have been a 'contender' right at the very top, especially in track and field sporting events.

I lost touch with Andy, although I once heard something about him living in Milton Keynes, close to where I used to live in the village of Cosgrove. Then, in 2012, at The London Olympics, a young man called Greg Rutherford, from Milton Keynes, won the Gold medal for the long jump. I saluted his victory and was even more elated when I found out a few days later that Greg was Andy's son. It seemed so fitting, so perfect. It is ironic how many great sports people had parents from the same field, or as encouraging and enabling supporters. Andy and Greg, I salute you both, father and son carved from the same metal and determination of spirit.

My sister, Celia, helped to carry the 2012 Olympic torch on its travels around the country. It was wonderful to gather as a family and see her run her stage to the cheers of the crowd. She did it in style, and it was fitting for Celia to have been chosen as one of the torch bearers, given all the hard work and effort that she had put in to helping other people.

The number of ex school kids who cheered her on was beautiful to behold. We all carry a torch of humanity within us in all that we do. Sometimes the greater glory is in our own hands, and in the next, it is in the hands of the following generation. We are plant, fruit and seed. When we keep growing and going, the light of our example can help others to keep going and growing themselves.

ACCEPTANCE AND LETTING GO

Every chapter of our lives has its pros and cons. Everything we do or don't do has an effect in the quantum field and on the quality of our lives, whatever age we may be. As Robert Holden likes to say: "It is never too late to be happy". We can make peace with our lot, as Morrie Schwartz did so remarkably when dealing with terminal illness. His exploits and life lessons about dying became the basis of the best-selling book, *'Tuesdays with Morrie'*, written by his friend and ex-student, Mitch Albom. If you have not read this book, I highly recommend that you do.

We can learn to sky dive at ninety or start a publishing company at sixty. You can write your first book at fifty-nine, *Rites of Man,* or sail across the Atlantic single-handed at fourteen as Mike Perham did. Age is a number. If we are capable, age doesn't make us too old or too young to do anything. As Del Boy from the TV show *Only Fools and Horses*[7] would say: "The world is our lobster." A dear friend, Trish Brunelle, wrote a famous quote from Goethe[8] in a journal she gave to me: "Whatever you can do or dream you can, begin it. Boldness has genius, power and magic in it."

Every day in any given moment we can have a change of heart, a change of plan, a change of mind. We can begin again, afresh, anew. We can let go of things that no longer serve us, commit to being better and chose to stack the odds in our favour. We can step out of a comfort zone, sing a song in public, write a book or phone someone up to apologise or reconnect. We can forgive to set ourselves and others free. We can learn to be wiser and if we keep growing for as long as we genuinely can, we will improve our lives and the lives of many others. We were born for this 'Hero's Journey'[9], so let's earn it and make the most of the time we have left by living wholeheartedly and giving it everything we've got.

LIFE LESSONS # 4

Φ Don't let the old one in. Stay young at heart and in spirit, and crack on.

Φ Fall down seven times and get up eight. Those who stay in the game the longest, get to reap the rewards of a life well-lived.

Φ Earn your life. Don't waste it, live it to the max and keep growing. It's never too late to be happy, take up a new hobby, a new career or make peace with your lot.

Φ Stay connected with important people who have influenced your life, and give it everything you've got, until the very end.

CHAPTER 5:

SOMETIMES, YOU'VE JUST GOT TO LAUGH

THE CUCUMBER

I'm fourteen and I'm stood in the family kitchen having a world-class argument with my seventeen-year-old sister, Celia. Things have become extremely heated and we are shouting fiercely in each other's faces when suddenly, the kitchen door bursts open and our mother walks in, slams her shopping basket down onto the table and yells at the top of her voice, "Stop it you two, now!" Protruding from the right-hand corner of the basket is a long large juicy cucumber, which my sister and I both stare at. Quick as a flash, Celia grabs the cucumber and wallops me across the top of my head. Now if you ever want to give someone a good smack, don't bother to use a cucumber, for when I opened my eyes after Celia's lightening thrust, there wasn't the slightest sensation of pain. I looked at her and she looked back at me. We both looked down at my sister's still clenched fist. All that was left in her hand was a tiny piece of gooey green mush hanging limply between her thumb and forefinger. We looked around the kitchen. The rest of the cucumber had vanished into thin air without a sound. There was no collateral damage or any debris to be seen whatsoever. I looked back at my sister and she looked at me and then we both turned to look at our mother. She was standing like a statue, open mouthed and frozen with the shock and surprise of what had just happened to her hard-earned shopping. I looked back at my sister once more, she looked at me and simultaneously we burst into laughter. On the other hand, our mother exploded with anger. Celia and I put our arms around each other and said; "it's all right Mum, we can't even remember what we were arguing about!" Laughter had brought us back together and the cause of the argument was completely forgotten. It took five minutes to find the rest of the cucumber, tucked neatly behind the refrigerator together with some dried-up vegetables and a pile of dust, and a further half an hour to stop sniggering. This only served to infuriate our mother all the more. A day or two later, after a long list of washing up and cleaning duties for the both of us, plus a trip to the greengrocers for me to get a replacement cucumber, our mother finally managed to smile again and we were forgiven. To this very day it is the best ending to an argument that I have ever been involved in, and no cucumber in my life, to date, has come close to rivalling the impact of that one.

SHAKEN AND STIRRED
I've just arrived at Les Menuires, part of a large and magnificent skiing area called 'Les Trois Vallées' in the French Alps, together with a motley crew of twenty-six men and women from the U.K. It's the mid-nineteen-eighties and we are here to ski fast and play harder. Its late afternoon, and we've checked-in to our hotel, collected our ski

equipment and are now headed to a bar for some pre-ski après-ski. I am twenty-five and it's a good time to be alive.

The restaurant we choose is a large noisy bar with a grand open space in front of a long bustling counter with several booths of varying sizes scattered around the perimeter. I am talking with three or four of the guys from our group, all around the same age, when we notice some rather pretty looking young women who are drinking shots and talking excitedly.

In order to be polite, what with being an English gentleman and all that, I saunter over to say hello. They smile and tell me that they are from Canada and that tonight is their last night in town before heading home, and so they are going to party all night long. Now it would have been extremely rude not to have joined them, so I suggested we all get a booth together on the far side of the bar, away from a large group of noisy guys who are busy getting drunk and being extremely boisterous. We learn that the they are soldiers from the British Parachute Regiment, who have come to The Alps to train and let their hair down.

As we begin to get to know one another, the drinks and conversation in our booth start to flow together and our levels of laughter rise to near Spinal Tap[1] proportions. Suddenly, one member of our group went, "shush", and we all stopped talking. "What's up?" I asked. He replied meekly; "The Second Battalion of the Parachute Regiment might hear us." There is instant uproar amongst our group and I voiced my thoughts: "So, what do you think they are going to do? Dig a tunnel and come up from under our seats, abseil down from the ceiling and land on our table, or rush across the bar and attack us with their bayonets?" This triggered even more laughter in our booth and the volume rose to eleven, causing the guys in the Regiment to look over at us. At this exact moment, another member of our skiing crew, who was sat in the next booth, stood up and looked over the partition to see what on earth was going on. As he did so, one of our new-found Canadian friends stared straight back at him and with a pointed finger exclaimed; "Oh my God, it's Sean Connery". I couldn't believe what I was hearing, so I had to correct her: "No it's not, it's Roger Moore." The whole booth burst into hysterical laughter and I fell off the bench holding my stomach, unable to breathe. Finally, I managed to climb back on to my seat and with a deep intake of breath, I said; "his name really is Roger Moore." The noise levels rose again with our laughter, and my stomach pains returned. By the time we had finally stopped laughing, it was my turn to go to the bar. A couple of soldiers asked me what on earth was going on. I told them, and they had a good laugh too. We ended up going to the same night club and a fantastic time was had by all.

LAUGHTER AS MEDICINE, HAPPINESS AS A PROJECT

Laughter is great medicine, something that kings, queens and tribal elders have known and utilised for centuries.

Jesters, clowns, heyokas and fools were hired to entertain and ease everyday fears and concerns by making people laugh at the craziness of life, boost morale and prevent us from taking ourselves too seriously. It is a basic truth that those who can laugh at themselves will never cease to be amused. Life is beautiful, precious, challenging and funny. It's easy to get caught up in trivialities or mini-me thinking, and forget that for the most part, we are the architects of both our happiness and our misery. As Eric Idle sang in the film *Monty Python's Life of Brian*[2], "You come from nothing, you go back to nothing, what have you lost? Nothing!" Laughter heals, it brings people together and it allows us to calm our frazzled minds from agitated thoughts. It is almost impossible to stay angry, cynical or miserable when you are having a really good belly laugh.

Many years ago, Dr Patch Adams[3] came to the U.K. and Ireland for a lecture and workshop tour. I immediately signed up for his event in London. He was a renowned teacher of clowning and the importance of using laughter and lightness in the practice of medicine. His life and work were the subject of the film *Patch Adams*[4] where he was played by the equally eccentric and brilliant Robin Williams. There were hundreds of people in attendance and Patch did not disappoint. Afterwards, I was persuaded to sign up for 'The Eight Week Happiness Programme' a five-day live event to be held over eight weeks in Oxford, England. It was to be led by Dr Robert Holden, who had been touring with Patch both as his 'warm up man' and sponsor of the tour. Robert ran an organisation in the U.K. called 'The Happiness Project' and had featured on a BBC QED Documentary, *How to Be Happy*, based on this training.

I arrived in Oxford and headed to the beautiful Linbury Building, adjacent to Worcester College, an historical campus that had partly inspired some of Lewis Carroll's writings, including that of *Alice's Adventures in Wonderland*[5]. As the programme unfolded, we began to dive into various exercises and conversations. For one of them, we were asked to lay down and form a circle in small groups, head to head. We were then played a recording of people laughing and a few titters began to arise amongst our group, dotted all over the room. We were encouraged to join in with the laughter but my inner cynic was not amused and despite a few attempts at a 'ha, ha, ha' or two, it was just not happening for me. It seemed too forced and too fake. Suddenly, one of the men, somewhere in the room, let out a loud guffaw and a woman snorted in response. This caused the same guy to laugh even louder which triggered the woman to snort even more wildly. Both of them had world class laughs. In a matter of seconds, I was joining in with what had become, more or less, the whole room nearly dying from the ridiculous laughter that was so contagious. I was in agony. I wiped away my tears and when the session finally came to an end, I was finally able to breathe fully once again. Who would have known then that five years later I would become the Business Manager and a Facilitator for Robert and The Happiness Project? But I did, and for seven years, boy did we have some fun and plenty more laughter.

BORN TO LAUGH

I was blessed to have been born with a twinkle in my eye and the ability to see the funny side of life came easily to me. Between the ages of eight and eleven I was often scolded and told to 'wipe that grin off of your face'. I developed crows-feet around my eyes before I was out of junior school and was called a 'Cheshire Cat'[6] by my headmaster for apparently 'smiling for no reason'. This was a similar crime to the one that Patch Adams had been charged with when he was at medical school. The truth was that I found plenty of reasons to laugh and smile at. Life can be absurd, but is more often than not our approach to life that is even more absurd. Laughter, and being excited and playful simply from the joy of being alive, is natural. It is only the worn down, the miserable or the controlling who would try to curb such youthful exuberance.

During my time with Robert and the happiness team, I ran a series of laughter workshops with a dear friend Ann Day. These culminated in the recording of a workshop for a live BBC Radio Oxford feature on happiness and the power of laughter to uplift and heal broken spirits. We shared funny stories in a circle and created mayhem by playing hide and seek in the BBC offices ahead of our interview with the shows anchor, Anne Diamond[7]. It was absolutely hilarious.

Over the years, I got to speak at several cancer care conferences in the U.K. about the importance of humour in palliative care, and how laughter was such a welcome relief even in the most difficult of circumstances. During a two-day happiness and success event that I ran in Ireland, the delegates and I shared some of our own hilarious experiences and stories in a local pub on the Saturday night. To this day, some of the situations and stories that were recalled are amongst the funniest that I have ever come across. There is so much comedy and hilarity in our everyday lives. Recounting our stories in workshops can be therapeutic as well as hilarious, due to the happy hormones that deep laughter produces, such as dopamine, oxytocin, serotonin and a variety of endorphins. These create a sense of well-being and pleasure in our bodies that is a great natural medicine for shifting the blues.

In a long-titled but seminal book *Anatomy of an Illness: As Perceived by the Patient*[8], its author Norman Cousins wrote about his miraculous recovery from a crippling and 'irreversible' disease. He tells us how he beat the odds by using his own powers of healing, together with a good intake of comedy. Cousins noticed that whilst in extreme pain that brought on insomnia, he had fallen asleep after watching a *'Marx Brothers'*[9] film. The same thing happened the following night after he watched another comedy movie. He believed he was on to something. As part of mobilizing our natural resources to overcome disease and illness, laughter truly can be powerful medicine.

FOOT IN MOUTH

Life is definitely a playground as much as it can be a school of hard knocks. If we want to have more fun and more joy in our lives, and improve our health and well-being, we have to remember to exercise our funny bone and lighten ourselves up in order to balance the more serious side of life. There can be great humour even in extreme circumstances which has led to so called 'gallows' humour and the irony that some of the most inappropriate situations for laughter often produce some of the funniest moments. Who doesn't know this?

It was an early autumnal grey Friday evening and my friend Sean and I decided to visit a local country pub for some beer and cheer by a warming fire. It was Sean's round, so he ordered two pints and passed one to me as he stood at the counter. I raised my glass to him, bowed and took a hearty swig. As I drank, Sean turned to a painting on the wall, pointed at it and asked the barman; "is that a portrait of Bill Hicks, the comedian?"

The landlord, without changing expression, replied: "No, that's a portrait of my recently deceased wife." I nearly choked and drowned as I desperately tried not to spit my beer all over the shiny wooden floor. Sean went for an apology: "Oh, I'm so sorry, I couldn't see properly from here" and I nearly died of a coughing fit, turning purple in agony, for the portrait was lit up by a giant spot-light. Bill Hicks would have loved every second of this interaction, for he knew that great moments of comedy sometimes come badly wrapped, as Robert Holden might have said.

Amongst my local friends who know of this incident, the pub has been aptly renamed as 'The Bill Hicks' in Sean and Bill's honour. Whenever we go back to this pub or think about the incident, we raise our glasses to the barman, to his wife and to Bill Hicks [10], a hilarious observer of life who was taken far too young.

COMEDY IN MOVIES

As Norman Cousins got to appreciate, movies are a great way to enjoy the parody of our lives and some of the absurdity that we create. I love the scene in the film *Beverley Hills Cop* [11] when Axel Foley arrives in Los Angeles. His laughter at the eccentric characters he meets is fabulous, as is the scene where he orders food for the cops who are supposed to be staking him out. No wonder the film was such a roaring success with its comedic approach to the murky world of gangsters and violence.

In the Alfred Hitchcock film *North by Northwest* [12], a wonderful scene occurs when Cary Grant's character is pursued into an elevator by two villains, both of whom have been trying to kill him. His mother does not believe his story and having bailed him out of jail is standing by his side in the elevator. Nodding with his head at the villains, Cary Grant points out to his mother the two gangsters that he had spoken about. She turns abruptly towards them and says: "Are you trying to kill my son?" They look at each other and then start to laugh. In seconds, the whole of the elevator, including Cary Grant and his mother, are in fits of laughter. It is comic genius from the film's director Alfred Hitchcock and epitomises how even in a dire situation, a moment of laughter can be created, even amongst protagonists. Sometimes laughter can even bring fighting, a grudge or an argument to an end, as it did with my sister, my Maori friend and I.

A MOMENT OF HUMOUR CAN BREAK THE ICE

I'm at the railway station on a busy early morning commute into London from the suburbs. To add to the usual rush, two trains have been cancelled. When one finally arrives, three train loads of passengers try to get on board. It is rammed, and I am having to stand in the middle of an aisle, squashed up against people on all sides. We set off and it feels like being in a small boat on rough seas with the train rocking from side to side and up and down as it goes. As we pull in to the next station, a large woman of ample proportions gets up and begins to fight her way through the throng to get off before the doors close and she misses her stop. As she approaches me, the train jolts to a final halt and she is flung straight into me, breasts first. She is apologetic and embarrassed, in equal measure, at her public assault upon me. I look at her and as we disengage, I say out loud; "It's a good job we all know each other." She and about five others close by laugh and the awkward moment is relieved with some lightness. We almost hug one another, again. The man to my right thanks me for bringing some warmth and cheer to a rather sombre carriage, whilst the rest of the commuters continue to stare blankly into their phones.

My favourite sports interview answer of all time is that given by the six-foot-seven former professional footballer, Peter Crouch. He was asked by a female interviewer, what he would have been if he hadn't been a footballer. Peter looked at her for a moment and responded with; "a virgin". A funny man, his droll response brought him to the attention of many. There is no doubt that such a witty retort can not only break the ice and lighten the mood but it can also bond us, for it is fun and healthy to be around light-hearted people who can lift our spirits and make us laugh. Long live our comedians and jokers.

SURPRISE, SURPRISE

After my introductory Enneagram session in London with Don and Russ, I signed up for their 'Part One' training, which led towards their teaching certification. With Lizzie, a colleague and friend from Success Intelligence, we travelled to the island of Andros for this program. It was an idyllic place to be studying this ancient and modern path to inner peace. The course was amazing, the group fabulous, and some great friendships were made.

On the way back to Athens and home, Lizzie and I

stopped briefly on the mainland, waiting for our ride to take us back to the airport. We had time on our hands, so we chilled on the beach for a while, and then had something to eat in a Taverna. Afterwards, I was enjoying a nice ice-cold lager and reading a book, whilst Lizzie read her magazine. Engrossed, I was only mildly aware that a trinket selling beach guy had come up to Lizzie to offer his wares. Suddenly, Lizzie said: "Hey Ian, have a look at this really cool Beretta-gun cigarette lighter" and handed it over.

I put my book down but held on to my nearly full pint of lager in my left hand. With my right hand, I picked up the lighter and pulled the trigger. Instantly, I received an electric shock. My beer shot out of my glass right up into the air. Incredibly, like a circus or magician act, I caught most of it back into the glass. Sadly, a big dollop of the ice-cold lager landed on the bare back of a young lady, sat behind me, wearing a tiny bikini top.

She reacted as if she had been shot, and so did Lizzie, who fell off her chair laughing. I apologised profusely, something I seem to have done a lot of in my life and in this book. After the fuss died down, and calm was restored, there was only one thing left to do: Buy the lighter and take it home. So, we did, and passed on the surprise and the fun. Shock is one of humour's greatest weapons, which is part of the reason why Cilla Black hosted a successful British television show called '*Surprise Surprise*' [13], which ran for seventeen years.

WHEN THE OCEAN CALLS

On a trip to Ireland to visit my friends Con and Eleanor at their beautiful home in West Cork, I travelled to the English Market in Cork City, where I bought a fine bottle of Châ*teau Lynch-Bage* [14] wine, named in part after my parental clan. My thinking was that it would be perfect for a special occasion once I got back home to the U.K., so I also purchased a couple of bottles of merlot for general quaffing during our evenings ahead. A day or two later, with Con's wife Eleanor away for a wedding, Con and I decided to head to The Fisherman's, a local inn in Union Hall and have a couple of jars before our supper. Once back home, Con began to cook dinner and so I opened one of the merlots. We chatted away with plenty of blarney and played some of our favourite music as we enjoyed each other's company.

Over dinner, we decided to open the second bottle of merlot, as the first one had gone down so well. Once we had finishing eating, we carried on listening to Bob Dylan and talked late into the night. Then, when the second bottle came to a sudden and abrupt end, we had a crisis. All that we had left was the *Lynch-Bage*, bought for a special occasion. We weighed up the pros and cons, and decided, wisely, that this was indeed the special occasion that it was meant for. Our reverie continued until around three-fifteen in the morning, when the *Lynch-Barge* was no more. Con suddenly had a brain wave; "let's go skinny dipping" and without hesitation, I said yes. At three-thirty am precisely, we got some towels and headed on down to the rocky cove.

The waters around the west coast of Ireland are not renowned for their warmth and at this time of year it was cold enough to 'freeze the balls on a brass monkey'. At the beach, Con dived straight in like a penguin hurling itself off of an iceberg, and splashed around whilst I stood at the water's edge shivering in the cold Atlantic sea breeze, wondering what on earth I had agreed to. Con told me that if I didn't get in now, then he would rugby tackle me into the icy waters. The thought of that just didn't bear contemplating, so I dived in. It was freezing and we were like 'Weebles', wobbling and slipping as we splashed about amongst the algae covered rocks, having decided to head back home for some warmth and a night cap. Suddenly, before we had a chance to reach our towels, a huge searchlight was shone down upon us from the large house at the end of the promontory, owned by Con's friend Pierre. Instinctively, I dropped to my knees, put my hands above my head, and in a strange French/German accent said: "Don't shoot. Don't shoot." Con behaved very differently. He jumped up and down on the spot, and like a naked leprechaun he shouted; "ahoy, ahoy. Come and join us. Come and join us." The light dimmed and then went out completely. I can only imagine that having been woken up at such an ungodly hour, Pierre had been expecting to see a bunch of noisy young holiday makers. Instead he was subjected to the sight of two naked gentleman of a mature age shouting and beckoning at him to join them. By the time Eleanor arrived back home, news of Pierre's ordeal had spread far and wide. As the door opened, Eleanor said: "Con Hurley! What have you been up to whilst I have been away"? It felt a bit like being in a Tom and Jerry cartoon, where we had been caught drinking cream from the refrigerator as the Housekeeper returned.

KEEPING YOUR EYE ON THE BALL

I was playing in a 'friendly' football match that was becoming far too serious and aggressive. Suddenly, the captain of the opposing team shouted at one of his own players to keep his effing eye on the ball. As soon as he had uttered this immortal sporting instruction, the ball was played straight to him and as he went to kick it, he missed it completely. I think everyone on the pitch, including the captain himself, burst into ironic laughter.

This one moment of comedy changed the nature of the game back to being the friendly it was supposed to have been. Sometimes, we have no choice other than to laugh. When that happens, life and the world seems a sweeter and better place to be. The more healthy and spontaneous laughter that we generate in our lives, the happier and more enjoyable will be our days.

LIFE LESSONS # 5
Φ Laugh and the world laughs with you. Weep and you weep alone. Exercise your funny bone, and try to look on the

bright side of life, as much as you can.

Φ Life is beautiful, precious, challenging and funny. There is so much to laugh and smile at. We all make simple mistakes, put our foot in it, and make a fool of ourselves.

Φ In times of trouble, some light relief can snap us out of darkness.

Φ Those who can laugh at themselves never cease to be amused. A real sense of humour includes the ability to laugh at ourselves wholeheartedly.

Φ Laughter is infectious and healthy. Make sure you catch some regularly.

CHAPTER 6:

AND THE OPPOSITE OF LIFE IS..?

IS THERE AN OPPOSITE TO LIFE?
It's a great question to contemplate because the answer affects the way that we experience the world and our identity and status within it. Modern cosmology and scientific studies are revealing that the universe is still being formed, a long and explosive birth of some fifteen billion years, with a possible two to three million of humanoid existence here on Earth. In eternity terms of course, that is no time at all.

To my mind, life doesn't appear to have an opposite, not as far as I can determine at least. Although life and death are often thought of as being opposing to one another, they seem to act as gateways through which life flows eternally, manifesting itself in different and mysterious ways throughout time, space and timelessness. If there had been just a single moment of absolute nothingness, then surely a total void would be all that there is today, tomorrow and forever. You and I, let alone our life-giving sun, the moon and all the stars in each and every galaxy, would not exist, not even as a twinkle in a heavenly eye. Yet here we are in a consumeristic society trying to understand how best to live, with varying degrees of success. Could we in fact be serial time travellers in relative interdimensional space, popping in and out of human form, and possibly the odd furry, feathery or extra-terrestrial body?

If we do live a multi-lifetime existence, it is quite possible that the game of humanity is to keep on reincarnating until every last one of us has mastered this physical plane of existence. Such a game might take many, many lifetimes, for we are like human butterflies who in one minute can flap our wings to create peace, joy and unity and in the next, flap them to create war, misery and destruction.

The sooner we all choose peace and unity the better, for then we can wave goodbye to the last vestiges of 'ass-soul' behaviour and enjoy the fullness of our true nature as fun-loving and peaceful souls, co-creators in the unfolding mystery of the universe.

OUR BELIEFS CREATE THE WORLD WE LIVE IN

Whatever your beliefs, it will be your relationship to birth and death that will determine many of the values and attitudes that you have towards how you live your life. Deep truths about who we really are can challenge us. Many people, myself included, catch themselves running away from confronting their fears and their potential, and therefore avoid spending time alone. A 'dark night of the soul', with its grief and its sorrow, can become a 'pearl' of transformation taking us into happier and wiser ways of being. Meditation and contemplation can reveal much about ourselves and our true nature. We might even get to appreciate that sorrow can become a friend, just like joy, one who is clearing us out for some new delight, as the Sufi poet Rumi wrote so beautifully in his time-less poem, *The Guest House* [1].

MY FATHER

I had a fraught relationship with my father, save for the first two or three years of my life and the last four or five of his. He had crafted a solid career for himself as a Chartered Mechanical Engineer, pushing himself through night school to overcome a tough upbringing. He had been born into one of the last of the old London slums with a father who was often drunkenly violent towards him, his mother and his sisters. Thankfully, my father wasn't a drunk and he never hit my mother, only my sisters and me. That finally came to an end when I locked my mother and sisters in the kitchen before turning to fight him, in what proved to be his final strike upon me. As a result, I left home temporarily. Whilst he never laid a finger on any of us again, his tongue continued to dish out a beating or two. Underneath it all, he actually had a good heart and was a man of moral courage and principle who seemed to be saddled with an inner rage at humanity's insanity and his own difficult upbringing. The older and wiser I became, the more I could understand and tolerate him, and in time, forgive and reconcile to the point that I could truthfully say that I loved him.

When my father died, my sisters and I each inherited a reasonably large sum of money which I dutifully spent on wine, women and wandering around the world. The rest, as the footballer George Best[2] famously stated, I just squandered. It was as if I couldn't accept my father giving me a helping hand, such was my deep wounding. Instead, I sought to spend the money rather than save or invest it, and although I had a lot of fun, it was neither a wise or prudent thing to do. One day, during this opulent phase, I was walking from my kitchen into the dining room, when I felt a violent shove in my back, the kind of thing you might experience in a game of rugby or American football. I turned around and there was no one there. No physical being that is. It wasn't an imaginary push, it was hard and forceful and it had an old familiarity to it. I knew instantly whose spirit it had to have been; that of my father. He was trying to get my attention and he certainly managed to do that, but I cracked on regardless. Like the man in Patrick Kavanagh's[3] poem, *On Raglan Road*; "I saw the danger, yet I walked along the enchanted way." Unable to stop myself, I packed a suitcase and headed for the airport. Four years later and I had practically blown the lot.

INTO THE ABYSS

When I returned from travelling in Asia I needed somewhere to stay, and my elder sister kindly gave me sanctuary in her family home in Hitchin. This proved to be a life saver, for not long afterwards I crashed into oblivion seeing no hope whatsoever of creating a worthwhile future, let alone a happy and successful one. My past shrivelled into a bitter catalogue of missed opportunities that amounted to a completely wasted life. All the successes and happy times seemed to vanish into meaninglessness such was the depth of my despair. My mantra became 'you've fucked it up' and I fell apart. If it hadn't been for my sister and her concern for me, I would have taken my life, I am sure, so low had I fallen. Thankfully, with the support of good friends as well as my family, I slowly began to regain my confidence and zest for life. A dear friend of mine recently told me how great it was to hear me laugh wholeheartedly once again, so crushed had I sounded during those dark days.

After a harrowing three years, I woke up ready to seize the day once again. I determined to make the most of the time that I had left, however long or short that would prove to be. I asked myself some existential questions: Why are we here together on Earth? Surely it can't be to squabble, fight and live as competitive individuals? Surely, we're not meant to be scared of death and worse, scared shitless about life? My breakdown had awoken something deep within me and I slowly began to regain my mojo.

MESSAGES FROM THE SPIRITS

As part of this renaissance period I decided to visit a local spiritualist church with the hope of getting a message of guidance via a psychic clairvoyant. I hoped that they would be a lot better than the 'can anyone take an old man in a wrinkled grey overcoat' type of mediumship that I had experienced previously. The medium of the day was a charismatic woman called Vivien who was funny as well as incredibly precise and accurate with the messages that she brought forth from those in spirit. Her style was fast paced, and she moved quickly around the room. She explained that this was to give as many spirits as possible a chance to get their messages across in the short amount of time that we had available. It was an impressive performance. Suddenly, she pointed at me, the man in the red ski jacket. Instead of giving me a message from my mother or another person in spirit, she said that she could see a beam of light radiating down onto me and that I was a writer, wasn't I? Having only written one book and just begun thinking about a second, I said; "well I guess I might be". She continued on, saying that she believed I had something of value to write about, if I took it seriously, and that those in spirit were shining their light to encourage me. She moved swiftly on to give her next message. I listened with great interest, whilst trying to take on board all that she had just said to me. One thing I noticed was that all of the spirits who came through her seemed to share one thing in common: They all reported that they were well and in a good place. None of them said that they missed Earth or that they hated their new existence and wanted to come back. I booked a personal reading with Vivien and headed off home to process all that I had witnessed.

A few weeks later, as I was having coffee with my friend Sean, I mentioned my experience at the Church and the follow-up reading that I'd recently had. Fascinated, Sean decided to come with me to the next monthly meeting at the Spiritualist Church. When I introduced Vivien to him, she said almost immediately, that his brother and father were standing right behind him. She added that his father was wearing his army uniform and that they were both smiling and wanted him to know that all was well with them and that he needn't be afraid of the future. Vivien was then asked to speak with someone else and left us. Sean wanted to know if I had told Vivien anything about his father and brother. I pointed out that he'd never shared anything about having a brother who had died or that his father had was once been in the Irish army. Sean was gobsmacked. Vivien's description had been completely accurate, and although they were physically dead, Vivien had somehow communicated with their essence. Like many of us, I had been taught that death was the final act and yet here were two former human beings showing up in spirit form, almost as if they were still alive. My mother and father had been the same in my one to one meeting with Vivien, just as many others have experienced for themselves. After such incidents, it is funny how we can get busy with our lives once again and forget about these fascinating anomalies. Death, it would seem, might not be the end of existence we have been taught. Heaven and Hell may actually exist. We'll just have to wait until our time comes to find out or go and see someone like Vivien.

SEEING THE DEAD

A former neighbour and good friend of mine, Neil Higson, was for many years the leading landscape architect for the city of Milton Keynes in the U.K. Neil was responsible for creating many of the city's most beautiful open spaces including the Tree Cathedral and the Labyrinth maze adjacent to Willen Lake. He was pivotal in the creation of The Circle of Hearts Medicine Wheel[4], a large standing stone circle close to a Japanese Buddhist Temple and Peace Pagoda, built to commemorate the bombing of Hiroshima and stand as a monument to world peace and an end to nuclear weapons.

Back in the nineteen-eighties, Neil and his wife Pirrko had a landscape architects business based from an old high street building along the ancient Roman road of Watling Street, in the ancient village of Stony Stratford[5]. In the days of horse drawn carriages, Stony, as it was known to the locals, had been a renowned coaching stop for travellers heading north from London. It became well-known for its 'Cock and Bull' stories and the 'Ride a Cock Horse to Banbury Cross' nursery rhyme.

At the end of a busy working day, Neil was chatting to a colleague at the bottom of a staircase that led to an empty floor above that was available to let. As they talked, Pirrko came out from their office to say goodbye to a client. As she did so, Neil and his colleague stood to one side to let an older gentleman in a long coat walk past them and up the stairs to the empty office. They imagined that he had come to view the letting and so they carried on talking. After their conversations ended and they started to get ready to leave, Neil said that he had better go upstairs to tell the visitor that they were about to lock up. Neil looked everywhere for the man, searching each room to no avail. Perplexed at having clearly seen the man enter the building and definitely not leave it, Neil switched the lights off and reluctantly locked up.

A few days later the matter was being discussed in a local pub when the landlord overheard the conversation and said that a man just as Neil had described had been seen on several occasions over the years and that he resembled a former shopkeeper who had died there long ago. Neil and his colleague looked at one another in astonishment, because to them, he had appeared as real as you or I when he had walked past them. Was it an echo from the past, a figment of their imagination or a visitation from a spirit caught between worlds?

It amazes me how many people I have spoken with over the years who have experienced something similar, or know of someone who has. And yet we seem, as a society, to dismiss such common occurrences because they don't fit in with the daily narrative and have not been scientifically verified. That is perhaps why we slip back so quickly into the every-day tick-tock world of modern life. As the Yoga Sutras of Patanjali[6] point out, 'misunderstanding is the delusion that stems from a false impression of reality'. We see only a tiny portion of the known visual spectrum, and yet we tend to believe that what we see with our human eye is the only reality that there is. The researcher, author and speaker Andy Thomas[7] explains in great detail in his book *Strange*[8], how so called 'supernatural' occurrences are much more common than we might realise. His extensive research and collection of people's experiences is impressive and eye opening as he comprehensively gives examples on a host of paranormal incidents from everyday life.

SPIRIT GUIDES AND STRANGE PHENOMENON
Many years ago, I was speaking with a wonderful friend and gifted medium called Lurline Paulwell-Tindle when suddenly, out of the blue, she said to me: "Did you know that you have two spirit guides standing right behind you and that they are laughing and smiling?" This was news to me. Lurline described them both as a tall thin man in his mid-twenties and an older smaller, bald headed stout fellow, who looked like he was from Asia. Apparently, they wanted me to know that they were here to support me in my life. I thanked them via Lurline and didn't really think too much about their appearance during the following days.

Six months later, I signed up for a vision quest in Sedona, Arizona. As part of the offering, I had a 'psychic painting reading' from a lovely man called Lawrence, who was also from the U.K. As Lawrence painted away and we talked, he said to me: "Two spirit guides are here with you." He then described them exactly the same as Lurline had done, and they were still smiling. I said jokingly: "Ah yes, they've been stalking me for some time now". In many ways I found this all a bit too much to take fully on board. Then, three or four years later, my sister-in-law, also called Vivian and known affectionately as Bibbly-Bobs, told me that there were two spirit guides standing by my neighbours' fence, trying to get my attention. I asked her if it was a tall fat bald headed man and a short skinny guy and she looked at me as if I was an idiot. "No", she said, "it's the other way around."

It was only when my friend and mentor Kath Temple [9] suggested that I call upon them, that I finally began to recognise that these guys were turning up for a reason, and I had been ignoring them. It must be so frustrating for spirit guides to deal with being ignored once they have made an appearance. Perhaps they have to resort to poltergeist activity to get our attention. For that is what started to happen to me.

COSMIC TRANSPORTATION

Following this last visitation, weird things began to happen with regularity. One such occasion, occurred when I was getting ready to travel to America. On the day of my flight from London Heathrow, I showered, and then in my rush to get ready in time for the taxi to take me to the airport, I forgot to put my crystal ring back on. I only realised that I'd left it behind when I reached the terminal building and it was too late to head back and retrieve it. Slightly annoyed, I headed for the check-in.

Two days after I had arrived in the U.S. I decided to iron my t-shirts, as they were crumpled from being packed inside my suitcase. Thanks to my Mum's tutelage, I am a meticulous ironer, so if I was ever asked to take part in an 'extreme ironing'[10] contest, then boy, any shirt of mine is going to be pressed properly, whether I'm hanging off of a rock face at Machu Picchu, or diving beneath the waves off of The Big Island in Hawaii. I'd just finished the last one and was putting the iron away, when suddenly, out of the middle of the ironed t-shirts dropped my ring, which then rolled slowly across the parquet floor to land at my feet, just as it had with Bruce Willis in the film *Sixth Sense*[11]. I had to pinch myself to make sure that the ring was real and that I was still alive.

There was no way this occurrence could be explained rationally for I had definitely left the ring at home in my bathroom. I had also ironed every part of every item so thoroughly, that a hidden ring would have revealed itself as I removed the creases from each t-shirt. If my ring had indeed been transported through time and space across the world, which was the only explanation I had left, then the chances were high that it had been one of my spirit guides who had pulled this off. How, is beyond our current scientific knowledge, at least that which has been shared.

BELT UP

Several years later, I was getting ready to go out for an evening meal and a few beers with some friends, so I chose a neatly ironed pair of brown jeans and put them on. My mother had also taught me to pee before I went out of the house on any journey, so I obeyed her ritual. As I left the bathroom, the top button of my jeans popped open. Dang, I thought, I can't be having that happen at the restaurant. So, I looked for my brown belt to match the jeans, but it was nowhere to be seen. I settled for a black one instead, and headed off to the café bar.

It was a fun evening and after a couple of Efes Turkish beers at Ziba's in Hitchin [12], I needed to pee once again. As I started to undo the black belt it seemed strangely tight. To my utter bemusement, underneath it and done up, there was my brown belt. I was wearing both. "No frickin' way", I said to myself. I would have noticed if had threaded one on top of the other, as it would have been so difficult to do. Again, this was an impossibility or else I was losing my mind. It had to be one of my spirit guys taking the piss once again, and making it more difficult for me to have one in the process. Spirit guide japes straight from the *Beetlejuice* [13] text-book.

I firmly believe that either one of these thrice spotted 'spirit guides', if not both, have probably been brothers of mine in another life time. Now, after all the years that have passed since their first appearance and with my thick curly dark brown hair having waved goodbye, I'm even starting to look like the short fat bald one.

Whenever I see or experience things that are out of the ordinary like this, it becomes far more difficult for me to believe or accept that death is the end of our lives.

LIFE CONTINUING AND EVOLVING

Over the years, I have felt a ley line and seen unidentified flying objects come in and out of physical existence. I've seen and experienced the strange and unexplained beauty of a complex crop circle and watched in awe as Hopi Rain Dancers danced and it rained on a clear, bright and blue Arizona spring day. I have seen a large black disc come into view and then disappear as if going through an invisible hole. All of these things I have experienced with others.

In the noughties, at a conference in Detroit led by Marianne Williamson [14], I was fortunate to meet a brilliant cosmologist, Brian Swimme [15], the author of *The Hidden Heart of The Cosmos* [15]. Brian reminded us that the more we immerse ourselves in the universe, with its interrelationships and energy exchanges, then the more we are likely to experience the joy of being alive as a unique and integral part of its existence. After all, we have the energy of the sun within us, a very good reason to be radiant and bright. With over three billion stars in just one galaxy, ours, the miraculous and majestic Milky Way, we can look out on a dark star-studded night as photons from the beginning of the universe that have finally reached us. And from where they have come from, if you were there and could look back in our direction, you would be experiencing the same thing as from here. Both places are at the beginning and the centre of the universe. Something intelligent and incredible is unfolding out of itself and we are at the heart of it all.

GIVING LIFE OUR BEST SHOT

Being a child of Mother Earth, God, The Universe, or however you prefer to describe yourself, is one heck of a ride. It is not dull even though sometimes we might get bored. If I am right, and life doesn't have an opposite, then just for today and for tomorrow as well, why not see how much love and merry mischief making you can conjure up to make our world a better place? If I am wrong, and life proves to be a one-shot deal, then we might as well give it everything we've got to make a difference for our children, if not for us. I'm up for both options, whatever the truth turns out to be, how about you?

LIFE LESSONS # 6

Φ How you view death affects how you live life. Value and respect life whatever your beliefs, and stay open for new information and knowledge.

Φ The supernatural is more natural than super. Keep your senses alert and chat with others. There's a lot more going than be are often aware of.

Φ Watch out for messages from beyond. We are being supported. If you experience something out of the ordinary, make a note, like a journalist, about all that just happened in detail. It can help remind you that there is more to life than we are usually aware of.

Φ We are made from starlight. Whilst you are alive in this body of yours, do everything that you can to make this world a better and brighter place.

CHAPTER 7:
SETTING SAIL FOR THE SHORES OF THE HEART

THE WORLD DOES NOT OWE YOU A LIVING
When I was seventeen and a student at Roundwood Park School in Harpenden, my chemistry teacher, Bob Anderton, taught me a tough yet powerful lesson that has stuck with me for life.

I didn't have an encouraging or supportive male role model to guide me in my formative years, so sometimes my innate and boisterous 'joie de vivre' could turn me into a *'Dr Jekyll and Mr Hyde'* [1] character of unruly and questionable behaviour. One such transformation led to a fellow classmate and I chalking graffiti of unpleasant images and personal insults about Bob onto the side wall of his house, which backed onto a public alleyway. On hearing the gory details of our 'street art', another of my classmates drew an amusing, albeit rude and cruel, cartoon of our misdemeanour onto a cardboard divider that I used to separate my biology 'A level' projects. His drawings were accurate in a funny and equally unfunny kind of way.

Over the next five semesters, I completely forgot about the whole incident, and so without thinking of the consequences, I handed in my biology projects as part of my final exam coursework. About a week or two later, after a chemistry lesson had just finished, Bob asked me to stay behind, as he would like to have a quick word with me. I had no idea what he wanted to speak about, until he produced my biology folder, opened it at the cartoon covered divider, and placed it onto the desk in front of me. As his Lab Assistant was leaving, she turned to ask Bob a question and so I had to wait to hear my fate whilst he talked with her, smiling and laughing as they spoke. As soon as she had left the room, his smile vanished and turned into an angry scowl as he ripped into me with full force about the upset the graffiti had caused to him, and his family. On being handed my folder, he said that his first reaction had been to call the police. He paused and stared at me for what seemed like an eternity, before saying that he was not minded to do so unless anything like that ever happened again. I assured him that it would not, by me at least, and I apologised profusely. Bob removed the divider and handed me back my folder, telling me to clean up my act. The whole incident brought me down to earth with a bang, for in my heart and soul I do not like causing harm or upset to anyone. I was rightly humiliated and a lesson was harshly learnt.

After the rollicking was over, Bob did not show any sign of holding a grudge against me, right up until my final exam. In fact, one day, as I was walking home, Bob offered to give me a lift into town and I accepted. We spoke about life in general and he asked me about my plans for the future, and then he said something profound: "Remember Ian, the world does not owe you a living. You have to make your own way in life. Follow your heart and then go out and make things happen so that you can achieve all that you want from life". I thanked Bob and he wished me good luck. It was the last conversation we were to have before I left school.

As he drove off, I thought about all that he had just said and the irony of the unfortunate circumstances that had led in part to him sharing this pearl of wisdom with me. Like Private Ryan, I would have to go out into the world and 'earn it.'[2] Although I can still remember the first line of the chemistry periodic table, thanks to Bob's tutelage, this was the greatest lesson that he ever gave me.

I bumped into Bob some thirty years later and he was genuinely pleased to see me, and I to see him, for I had heard that he was not in the best of health. He asked me what I was up to and smiled as I explained and thanked him for his wisdom from all those years ago. He shook my hand and wished me good luck once again. It was to be our last meeting, for a short while later I heard the sad news that he had passed away. As with every soul who has touched my life, I hope that we will meet again, and if there proves to be a next time with Bob, it will most definitely be without chalk.

YOUR LIFE, YOUR VOYAGE
I have shared with you some of the most important lessons

about life that have been meaningful to me over the past fifty years. You will have your own. Some of them may be similar to mine, and others very different. Every one of us could have an award-winning film made about our lives and all that we have gone through to make us the person that we are today. It might be a soap opera, a thriller, a war movie or a rom-com. It might contain elements of all four. We are the co-director, writer and starring actor in our own lifetime adventure, and our heroic future, as they say, is yet to be written.

Our lifetimes are great explorations, and I love the analogy of each one being a journey, a voyage. As master of our human vessel, we ultimately decide the beliefs and resources we take on board our minds, what is no longer relevant for the next leg of our journey, and where we will be sailing to next. We might find ourselves sailing with others in one moment and then sailing alone in the next. When we take full responsibility for the helm, we give ourselves a far better chance of leading a fulfilling and rewarding life. Choosing a good crew to sail with can make our lives a lot easier, just as choosing a motley crew can make them more difficult.

I once heard a story about a small boy who was having the nightmare of being chased by a big scary snarling monster. As the monster got closer and closer the boy tripped and fell to the ground. Feeling the monster's hot putrid breath on the back of his neck, the boy turned around sharply and looked up at the monster, which was staring menacingly down at him. The boy cried out in anguish: "What are you going to do to me?" and the monster replied: "I don't know, it's your dream." And so, it is with our lives, for we get to choose the next move.

A SHIP FOR ALL SEASONS

On my Egyptian excursion in 2016, I visited an incredible artefact that had been discovered in 1954: Khufu's Solar boat[3]. This is a barque that was made for this world and for the next. With an ingenious design, this boat had been created in sections that could be dismantled and carried across land to be reassembled at the next navigable location, saving the crew a longer and more arduous route. Held together by tightened ropes, the wooden sections expanded when placed back into water, making the boat watertight and ready to sail once again.

This solar boat is similar to our human vessel made from mind, body and spirit, and bound together by the knowledge, beliefs and experiences that we have gathered over the years. If one section fails or falters, we can sink to the bottom in an instant. Every now and again it is a good idea to pull into port and take stock of our lives. We all need some time out to stay healthy and assess how things are going.

Most highly successful people turn to a coach or a trusted advisor to help them improve their ability and make their best judgment calls. With such guidance to hand, we can get to see alternative viewpoints and explore other options that we might not have considered. If we go through life doing it all by ourselves, we can end up making mistakes and missing out on better opportunities. Once we have total clarity and know exactly what we want, we are in a much better position to make the smartest decisions for getting us there.

PIRATES AND THREE PEARLS OF WISDOM

In my early forties, I took a road trip around Florida with three friends from England. We had lots of fun driving across this fabulous state, which offers so much to be seen.

As a kid growing up in the nineteen-sixties, I loved to watch the 'missions to the moon', and so the prospect of visiting Cape Canaveral was an absolute dream, as was visiting the Everglades, Miami, with its art deco buildings, and the area of Naples on the western coast. Once there, we stayed in a motel run by a witty hotelier who was raised in Chicago. After we had checked in, I asked him for directions to a particular restaurant that we fancied eating in. He gave me the directions in great detail, and so I asked if he could repeat them one more time to make sure I had heard them correctly.

He fixed me with a steely gaze and said: "You Brits used to rule the seas, now you can't even find your way round a few goddamn blocks. No wonder you lost your Empire." We laughed and he told me again.

A day or two later, as we were thinking of going further up the coast to Fort Lauderdale to celebrate the New Year, I decided to take my chances and seek his advice once more time. He said: "Listen boys, Naples is where people come to retire. Where you are thinking of going is where their parents go to retire. You want to head down to the Keys. That's where the action will be." So off we went to spend New Year's Eve in Islamorada in the company of *'Big Dick and The Extenders'* [4], legendary entertainers of the day.

When our trip had come full circle, we headed back to Orlando and decided to be proper tourists, or 'grockles', as John Alexander West loved to say. We headed to Universal Studios [6] and then onto Disney World [7]. Here, there was a Pirate Ship ride with a long queue to get to the boat. Waiting in front of us was a young girl with her mother. We could see that she was fascinated with our very strange British accents, which to her small ears, sounded a little bit like that of pirates. Seizing the moment, Doug introduced himself as Cap'n Percy, me as Cap'n Lynch, and the other guys as Cap'n Bailey and Cap'n Tompkins, rrrrrrrr. It was a fun moment of interaction and we played our part in adding some extra excitement and entertainment to this young person's experience. Peter Ustinov and Dean Jones, stars of the Disney movie 'Blackbeard's Ghost' [8], would have been proud of our performances.

I recently attended a three-day event, celebrating the twenty-fifth anniversary since the publication of Robert Holden's best-selling book *Shift Happens* [9]. As we began the program, my name came out of 'the hat' for a walk-through exercise in front of the group. This triggered the old 'I knew it was going to be me' thought, followed by an 'oh shit', rather than an 'oh shift' response. For this exercise, Robert handed me three pearls and asked me to share with the group what each one might represent in my life today. With a deep intake of breath and a heavy sigh, I overcame my inner critic to reveal what they were and where I was with each one. This was both a privilege and an ordeal at the same time, for the aim of the exercise was to look for gifts that can arise after experiencing a 'dark night of the soul'. I still had some lingering sorrow from my breakdown and from my current circumstances not being as I would want, but I had also come to appreciate the value and blessings that I had gained from sinking so low. Sorrow and humility had wiped away some more rough edges and enabled me to see in bright lights what was truly important to me. Where there are pirates and dark storms, sometimes there will also be pearls.

I SECOND THAT EMOTION
I have only scratched the surface of the raw emotion that I felt on some of the best and worst days of my life that I have shared with you in this book. Such deep feelings make the human experience so painful and yet so wonderful. They can lift us up to where we belong or cut us down like a scythe. They fuel our songs and our poems, our prisons and our graveyards. It is worth getting to know them well, no matter how uncomfortable they can appear to be when we are in the thick of things. Leonard

Cohen in his song *Anthem* [10] says it perfectly; "There is a crack, a crack in everything, that's how the light gets in." A mistake, an accident or a fall can be the perfect 'crack' that we need to break us open for something more beautiful to be revealed.

Life is a wibbly wobbly adventure of self-discovery, self-actualisation and self-remembering. When we die, I personally believe that we will be heading home to a mystical realm of our pre-birth existence, a place that some call Heaven, some call Source and some call Hell. Thankfully, we don't have to die to experience our true nature, but we do have to let go of the insignificant and the chitter chatter of nonsensical irrelevance. We do have to find ways to quieten our fears and learn to be happy and comfortable with being in our own company, alone. Then, once we have come to a place of peace within ourselves, we can, as Christy Moore sings so majestically in the song *The Voyage* [11], set sail for 'the shores of the heart.'

INTO THE MYSTIC

In the process of writing '*Rites of Man'*, I decided to work on the chapter called '*The Ancestors'* whilst on a trip to Ireland, the home of my paternal great grandparents. I had travelled across the country to Dingle and was enjoying the beautiful countryside in this part of the world. As I drove around the coast line, I found the perfect spot to finish the chapter, close to a café overlooking the Atlantic Ocean, and so I parked up. I walked a short distance from the café and sat on a rock facing the sea. As I began writing the summary, something very different began to emerge. Instead of my usual wrap up for each topic, an invocation and calling from the past to the present came to mind. It was as if I was being guided by my own ancestral lineage written into my flesh and bones, coupled together with the spirit of the land, here on this 'Emerald Isle'. Here is that summary:

'Imagine if we were all seeded from the stars and our spirits could move across the generations. We would then be able to build bridges of respectful kindness to one another, heal old wounds, and create a lineage as one human family upon this earth. We would unshackle the true joy and beauty of being men (or women) in all our glory, dancing with 'The Ancestors'. We are the people that we have been looking for to lead the way. We carry the torch of humanity within us, until the day comes when we too become the ancestors of tomorrow and pass it on'.

It is the journey to opening our hearts fully to one another that is one of the biggest and greatest undertakings in life. I have cried tears of sorrow and tears of joy in equal measure. Sometimes it's been hard to tell the difference. Movies have caused tears to flow for the people on the big screen that I was not able to shed for myself. Music has given me solace in times of difficulty and made my body dance in ecstasy with a mind of its own. The 'paranormal' and 'supernatural' has shown me that there is a lot more going on around me than I am usually aware of. There is something much bigger, and yet invisible, holding everything together, and I think there is no finer song to remind us of that than *'Into the Mystic'* [12] by Van Morrison.

THE CALLING

On a birthday treat to San Diego I was very fortunate to spend time with the wonderful musician Shawn Galloway[13]. Shawn helped me to birth my *'Rites of Man'* book and he set the tone for the five-day coaching program I was attending by singing a beautiful and potent song called *'The Calling'*. This song contains a powerful chant that cries out to everything and anything, but most especially to our hearts. For the closing of this powerful event, Shawn invited us all to join him in singing this chant. As with a Haka or a passionate anthem, *'The Calling'* is an invocation to bring divine light into our hearts for all that we are about to do. When we sang together at full volume, the vibrations of sound and waves of joy reverberated through us. It truly was a spine-tingling experience and we all felt as one. I strongly suggest that you get a hold of this song, turn up the volume, and join in with this chant for yourself. It contains something powerful and primal that our body seems to know.

If we bring our life lessons into the light of conscious awareness and sit with them, giving ourselves the grace of our own presence and company, our true calling can speak to us. When we shed unkind, untamed and unwanted thoughts, when we listen in silence, there can be great wisdom and deep peace waiting to take their place. Our spark for life can be reignited and we can go out into the world anew. We are here to learn, here to grow, and here to have some fun. We are not here to struggle or bumble along. We are here for a bigger purpose; to bring love and peace into the world. That is our biggest calling, our greatest challenge, and our most important work. May you be a light in the world, may love fill your sails, and may the winds of time and transformation take you onwards to happiness and fulfilment, and then back home once again, into 'The Mystic'.

LIFE LESSONS # 7

Φ The world does not owe you a living. Take full responsibility for your actions and commit to your goals, dreams and chores with passion and purpose.

Φ You are master of your own ship. It's your choice as to how and where you set sail for.

Φ Nail love to your mast and let it guide you every step of the way.

Φ You carry the torch of humanity in all that you do. It took a universe to explode into being to create you. Your greatest legacy will be made from your kindness, generosity and wisdom of deed and doing. Make it count.

EPILOGUE:
A NEW CHAPTER BEGINS

COMING BACK FROM THE DARKNESS OF DESPAIR

From those hideous days and nights of despair when I so nearly gave up, I have huge compassion for anyone who is suffering with a mental and emotional collapse. I also recognise just how lucky I am to have had a sister like Celia, and a brother-in-law like Stuart. I would have given up and gone, I am sure, without their love and assistance. If you had told me five years ago that I would fall into a place utter hopelessness, I wouldn't have believed you. That has shown me that anyone could fall prey to a mental anguish so strong that thoughts of letting go of life become more appealing than staying alive and facing up to things. What I have also found, is that by working diligently to replace negative thoughts with ones of real determination and purpose to change things up, something new and hopeful can be created despite the pain and difficulty.

I am much more accepting of myself than I have ever been. I am more open and more focussed on what I would like to create and experience, but with some non-attachment to the outcomes, which is fascinating. I am staying vigilant and feeding the 'wolf of love'[1]. I just have to remember Morrie and dig in, if I am challenged.

When I was studying restorative justice, a wonderful

man told a story of how he had helped to curb a spate of young male suicides in his community, He got a group of lads together and asked each one of them to commit to staying alive for the next twelve months by writing it on to a flip chart, to be kept on the wall of the centre. Everyone one of them signed up. It worked, and no one else took their lives. I commit to staying alive too.

HOW LOVE COULD CHANGE OUR WORLD
I am a romantic, and I like to think about ideas that could change our world into a better place. Some of them are small and local, and some are almost ridiculously large, but I dream on.

The 'Summer of Love' of 1967 touched me musically and spiritually as I have mentioned, and I have often thought that a second, larger 'Summer of Love', might help to counter some of the fear and anxiety that seems to be so rife in our world today. Starting in the Southern Hemisphere and sweeping around the globe, like a Mexican Wave as it reaches the Northern Hemisphere, an expanded 'Summer of Love' would be amazing. All that it needs is one spark of genius to ignite it, and the will for people to come together and share some great music and creative enterprises together from all over of the globe.

Perhaps even more boldly, we could create a 'Moment of Unity', where all who felt called, irrespective of viewpoint, came together at exactly the same moment in time, for three minutes of solidarity and connection, simply for being a member of the human race, standing together as one in that same moment of time. How powerful and amazing could that be? How powerful would a global chant be at the end of it? If you are in on one or both of these ideas, let me know, and let's get it on.

SITTING ON TOP OF THE WORLD

One of the most heart-warming workshops I have facilitated, was a free event held in California in support of a wonderful organization that mentors young lads. My friend John and I worked out a lovely schedule of activities to inspire and entertain the boys. We played two lies and a truth, put them into teams for some light challenges and ended the day with a sharing around an open fire. At lunchtime, one of the lads, the youngest, posed a question to me. "Which would you rather choose, a year on the top of a mountain without the Internet, or having to fight fifteen zombies?" I answered: "Let me think about that" and then I responded: "I tell you what, if you can make it two years on top of the mountain without the Internet, I'll fight thirty zombies for the opportunity to go and live there." The young lad looked at me as if I had gone completely mad and said: "Don't be stupid, no one could survive for two years without the Internet." It was a priceless moment, so intriguing, so amusing, and the other guys, all of a similar age, laughed and said they would happily join me on the zombie battlefield. They were a great bunch of kids and a great bunch of guys to spend time with and we all enjoyed a thoroughly fabulous time together.

As I begin the eldership years of my life, I am upbeat, largely because of the horrors that I faced three or four years ago and the reset that I am now undertaking as a result. Like the heroes who gave their lives for our freedom in the second world war, my generation is beginning to become a dying breed. Born in the days of black and white telly and transistor radios, whistling kettles and small grocery stores rather than giant supermarkets, we have an experience of a different world, where the latest technology was a cassette player. I love the idea of singing the Sex Pistols song *'Pretty Vacant'* [2] in a care home when I am ninety-five, jumping up and pogoing with my Zimmer frame or walking sticks, dribbling rather than spitting. The world today is more complex, but thankfully, there is still so much beauty and opportunity to enjoy in life. The younger generation spur me on to play my part and not quit before my body clock says its time to go. I still have some fuel left in the tank.

The principles that I have shared with you in these seven lessons are timeless. You can't go too far wrong if you are at peace with yourself, have a good sense of humour, look out for others, keep on growing, see life as an adventure and only moan here and there in the right places. If you stay true to such principles, learn from your experiences, have a clear vision of what you want for your life and keep your heart open to love, I think you have pretty much smashed it.

As for me, I'm going to see where my love and help are most needed and make the most of this day and any bonus days that come my way. Thank you taking time to read about some of my life to date, and the sense that I have tried to make from it all. I hope that it has been of value and entertainment to you. Maybe at some point you'll share some of your wisdom with me, either in this lifetime or in the next, for at a soul level, I imagine that I'll be seeing you around, one way or another. Until then, be safe, be wild, be wise, and be true to the calling of your heart.

NOTES AND REFERENCES

PROLOGUE

1 BBC2 was first broadcast on the 20th April 1964. At the time it was a big deal, a third television channel. Heady days.

2 The Beatles song 'She Loves You' was released in August and September 1963 in the UK and USA respectively. In the USA this song was one of five Beatles songs that took all top five positions in the charts in April 1964. It was the biggest selling single of the nineteen-sixties.

3 The Monkees TV Shows ran from 1965 to 1968. They were a blast to watch.

4 The Summer of Love actually began in January 1967. As many as 100,000 people descended on the areas of Haight-Ashbury and Golden Gate Park in San Francisco as word spread of the counter culture community gathering there. It is a joy to visit the area today, and The Golden Gate Park is one of my favourite parks in the world.

5 Belladonna. Atropa bella-donna is more commonly known as 'Deadly Nightshade'. As with many plants, it has medicinal properties and is farmed for them. Not a good idea to try a berry.

6 Yellow Submarine was released in August 1966 and became the title of a subsequent Beatles film released in 1968. It is worth listening to the Beatles' recordings of this song, as it developed out of something much more melancholic.

7 Sugar Sugar, was a hit single from The Archies, a fictional group from an animated US TV series managed by Don Kirschner, who had previously been involved with The Monkees.

8 Woodstock – 15th to the 17th August 1969 attracted an audience of more than 450,000 with many more unable to get there, blocking roads and causing huge traffic jams for days. Today the site of the festival is home to Bethel Woods Center for the Arts. It was a pilgrimage to go visit the site and watch a concert there.

9 Marc Bolan was the lead singer of a psychedelic folk-rock band called Tyrannosaurus Rex, abbreviated to T.Rex. Formed in 1967, the band became popular in the era of 'Glam Rock'. Marc was

known for his corkscrew hair, and so was I.

10 The Mercury space programs ran from 1958 to 1963, the Gemini space programs began in 1963 and concluded in 1966, to be replaced by the Apollo Moon Missions. The Apollo missions captured the western world's attention, and the race to the Moon was on. It was riveting television.

11 Star Trek exploded onto our TV sets, dwarfing everything else with its high tech sets and gadgetry. It captured the public excitement in the nineteen-sixties for space exploration. The first episode aired in 1966, though we had to wait until 1969 in the UK for the series to be shown on the BBC.

12 'Stig of the Dump' is a novel by Clive King, and first published in the UK by Puffin Books in 1963. It has now become recognised as a children's classic. Stig is a caveman who has survived living in a chalk pit in The Downs of England. The location is kept secret, as it is believed he is still there. ISBN 978-0-14-034724-1

13 Steve McQueen played Captain Virgil Hilts in the 1963 movie *The Great Escape,* who longs to escape from the German POW camp. He also played the lead character of 'Papillon', Butterfly, in the 1973 movie of the same name, who is imprisoned on Devil's Island in French Guiana and longs to escape. Standing in the playground at Moreton End was just the same to me as a small boy of eight.

14 One Foot Island, Tapuaetai, is one of 22 islands that make up Aitutaki atoll of the Cook Islands. It is 570 metres long and roughly 210 metres wide. In 2008, at the World Travel Awards, it was named 'Australasia's leading beach.'

15 Robinson Crusoe, is a novel written by Daniel Defoe first published in 1719. It contains a description of "The island of despair' off the coast of Venezuela where Crusoe finds himself marooned.

16 John Lennon's song *Beautiful Boy* was released in 1980 as a track on his Double Fantasy album, which proved to be his last. The song includes the lyric 'life is what happens to you when you are busy making other plans' which is tragically poignant.

17 Ralph C Smedley formed the first Toastmasters club in 1924 to help people learn the art of public speaking. It is now an International organisation and I highly recommend it to anyone who wishes to improve their speaking skills and have some fun doing so.

18 *Schools Out* was a 1972 number one hit in the UK for Alice Coop-

er, and an anthem for kids at Roundwood at that time.

19 The Open University is based in Milton Keynes, England. It was established in 1969 and allows students to gain a Hons Degree, and other qualifications, without the need to attend college full-time.

20 *Rites of Man* was published in 2020. It is a book with a separate 70 card oracle deck for men. ISBN 978-1-9993529-8-1. You can find out more at *www.ianlynch.net*

21 *Tuesdays with Morrie* was written by Mitch Albom and published in 1997. ISBN 0385484518. It is a beautiful book about life and death that I highly recommend.

CHAPTER 1: ONLY MOAN IF YOU'RE MAKING LOVE

1 *Flight Plan* is a book by Brian Tracy. ISBN 978-1-57675-497-9, Berrett-Koehler Publishing, 2008.

2 *Don't Sweat the Small Stuff* is a wonderful book written by Richard Carlson – Hodder & Stoughton 1997 ISBN 0 340 70801 8.

3 Mark Matousek *https://markmatousek.com/* Mark is an excellent teacher and brilliant writer. I highly recommend his book

4 The Esalen Institute. Go there, it's a stunning place to take a course or two, maybe with Russ Hudson.

5 *Rites of Man* was published in 2020. It is a book with a separate 70 card oracle deck for men. ISBN 978-1-9993529-8-1, You can find out more at *www.ianlynch.net.*

6 Lazy Sunday is a song by The Small Faces. It was released in 1968. It contains the lyric 'he mustn't grumble'. Check out their other work too.

7 'The whinging poms' came to being after the second world war when Brits could seek passage to Australia for £10. Some of them complained once they got there, and it became a disparaging phrase which is still used today. I'm not complaining.

8 Monty Python and The Holy Grail is a 1975 movie about King Arthur and his knights interspersed which includes the infamous scene with The Black Knight, Guardian of The Bridge.

9 A 'Hangi' is a traditional Maori method of cooking food using heated rocks buried in a pit oven.

10 The 'Hongi' is a traditional Maori greeting of rubbing noses together.

11 A 'Wharenui' is a traditional Maori communal and meeting house.

12 Haka's are ceremonial dances in Maori tradition, often performed in a group and with vigorous movements.

13 Kathrine Switzer. *https://www.therunningweek.com/post/kathrine-switzer-pioneering-womens-running-and-changing-history*

14 Zig Ziglar was a motivational speaker of the highest order. You can read some of his awards and accolades here. https://www.zigziglaraward.org/who-was-zig

15 Ray Clemence. You can read the write up by Jim White if you go to this link: *https://www.pressreader.com/ireland/irish-independent/20201116/282772064106673*

CHAPTER 2 STACK THE ODDS IN YOUR FAVOUR

1 Bananarama were formed in London in 1980. They were an 'all girl' pop band who had huge success.

2. Steve Wright was a UK Radio Presenter who had an afternoon radio show that had a huge following with a variety of made up characters, including *Mr Angry*.

3 Thomas Huxley was a biologist and anthropologist who advocated Charles Darwin's theory of evolution.

4 You can find out all the latest about Robert's work by signing up to his newsletter or visiting *https://www.robertholden.com/*

5 I highly recommend checking out Russ's work on the Enneagram. You can catch up with Russ via his website and sign up for his insights and monthly presence practice: *https://russhudson.com/*

6 John Alexander West was an archaeologist and 'revolutionary' writer on Egyptian history. He was also a wonderful and charismatic human being. His book Serpent in the Sky. The High Wisdom of Egypt, ISBN 9780835606912, is ground-breaking, with his evidence of water-erosion at The Sphinx fascinating, as was everything he taught and lectured on. It was a joy and an honour to spend time in Egypt with John. RIP John Alexander West.

7 The USS Enterprise, often referred to as the 'Starship Enterprise', was the command vessel of Captain Kirk in the nineteen-sixties TV series Star Trek and continues to be used in other film and media work.

8 Robert Baden-Powell was a British army officer who formed the

Boy Scout Movement in 1910 and The Scout Association Royal Charter of 1912.

CHAPTER 3 HERE TO HELP

1 Johan Cruyff was a Netherlands football player and coach, 1947 -2016. He is considered by many to be one of the greatest players of all time.

2 John Cremer – Improv: Enjoy Life and Success with The Power of Yes, November 2009, Eldamar Ltd, ISBN 978-0955391736

3 A Course in Miracles – Foundation for Inner Peace 1996, ISBN 0-670-86975-9

4 The Gunfight at The OK Corral of 1881 in Tombstone Arizona pitted lawmen and cattle rustlers in an epic battle that epitomises the days of the 'wild west'.

5 The University of Cranfield is situated just north of Bedford, some fifty miles north of London. You can read about the University here: *https://www.cranfield.ac.uk/*

6 Mr Burton is a 2025 film starring Toby Jones as Mr Burton and Harry Lawtey as Richard Burton.

7 The Titanic Museum is built on the site of the former Harland and Wolfe shipyard, which was once a major employer in the area. It is worth a visit to pay homage to our fellow humans who lost their lives in such a tragic way.

8 Robert Norton is an outstanding musician. He is the keyboard player with Curved Air, a renowned British Prog Rock band of note. His meditational music is sublime. You can purchase Robert's music at bandcamp: *https://robertnorton1.bandcamp.com/.*

CHAPTER 4 - KEEP GROWING TO THE END

1 *'Don't Let the Old Man In'* is a 2018 song by the American country music singer Toby Keith and featured in Clint Eastwood's movie *The Mule*, released in the same year.

2 'Where Eagles Dare' was a 1968 film starring Richard Burton and Clint Eastwood. As was the case in the days of the old-style cinemas before video, older films would be reshown regularly and it would have been 1972 that I went to Harpenden Cinema to watch this film.

3 'Saving Private Ryan' is a 1998 Steven Spielberg film starring Tom Hanks with Matt Damon as Private James Ryan. It charts the heroic

deeds by a group of soldiers to rescue Private Ryan and bring him home.

4 *Reasons to Stay Alive* by Matt Haig is a book that I never knew would play a part in my own struggle to stay alive. It charts his own depression and his strategies for not giving up. I highly recommend this book. You never know if one day you might need it. ISBN 9781782115083.

5 Morning Pages is one of the most powerful tools for downloading deeper subconscious desires and fears. It is a great way to unleash creativity. You can read about Julia Cameron's work at *https://juliacameronlive.com/*

6 *Enjoy Yourself* is a song written by Carl Sigman and Herb Magidson that was published in 1949. It has been covered by many famous singers and bands such as Doris Day, Bing Crosby, Jools Holland, The Specials as well as The Ska Souls.

7 *Only Fools and Horses* was a British sitcom that ran from 1981 to 1991 with Christmas specials until 2004. It was about a couple of ambitious market traders as they attempt to make 'a million'. Del Boy was played by David Jason with Nicholas Lyndhurst as Rodney. It is consistently voted into the top ten all-time greatest British comedy shows.

8 Johann Wolfgang von Goethe was a German polymath who is seen as one of the most influential writers in the German language. His body of work is immense and he has been described as a poet, a playwright, a novelist, a scientist, a statesman, theatre-director and critic.

9 A Hero's Journey was made popular by Joseph Campbell building on work by Otto Rank and Lord Raglan. Campbell's brilliant work continues to influence a new generation through his detailed models and comprehensive writing on the subject. Robert Holden also teaches Joseph Campbell's work, so do check that out, and if you haven't already done so, do read Campbell's book *The Hero's Journey*.

CHAPTER 5 - SOMETIMES YOU JUST GOT TO LAUGH

1 *This is Spinal Tap* was a 1984 movie directed by Rob Reiner starring Christopher Guest, Michael McKean and Harry Shearer. It charts a fictitious British rock band on a comeback tour to the US, including the infamous 'we can go to eleven' scene.

2 Monty Python's Life of Brian movie was released in 1979. It ends

with the song 'Always Look on The Bright Side of Life' where my quote is from.

3 Dr Patch Adams is a peace activist, clown and doctor. You can read about him and The Gesundheit Institute on his website: *https://www.patchadams.org/patch-adams/*

4 *Patch Adams* was a 1998 movie about Dr Patch Adams starring Robin Williams.

5 *Alice's Adventures in Wonderland* is an 1885 children's novel by Lewis Carroll, a mathematics don at Oxford University.

6 The Cheshire Cat is a fictional character in Lewi's Carroll's book Alice's Adventures in Wonderland and not lost on me when I was in Oxford with The Happiness Project.

7 Anne Diamond OBE, is a British journalist and broadcaster who rose to fame on morning time television in the UK. She has been active in this field since 1979. It was a joy to be on her BBC Oxford show.

8 *Anatomy of an Illness: As Perceived by the Patient* by Norman Cousins was published in 1979. It illustrates the power of humour and patient participation in care, as factors that increase recovery chances.

9 The Marx Brothers were an American comedy troupe who made fourteen movies as well as success on Broadway. There famous films include Duck Soup, A Night at The Opera and Monkey Business.

10 Bill Hicks was an American stand-up comedian and satirist who began working in clubs at just sixteen years of age, such was his confidence and genius in this field. He sadly passed away with pancreatic cancer at the age of 32.

11 *Beverley Hills Cop* was a 1984 movie starring Eddie Murphy, which shot him to international stardom.

12 North by Northwest is a 1959 soy thriller directed by Alfred Hitchcock starring Cary Grant, Eva Marie Saint and James Mason. It features many famous scenes not least the climatic struggle on Mount Rushmore.

13 The premise of *Surprise Surprise* was to play pranks and catch members of the public out, and reunite people with long lost friends or family members.

14 Chateau Lynch-Barge wine was part founded by Thomas Lynch,

138 ONLY MOAN IF YOU'RE MAKING LOVE...

a descendant from the tribes of Galway, in the French village of Bages. Check out your local wine merchants to find a bottle. If you are successful, please invite me round. I'd like to savour a glass.

CHAPTER 6 - AND THE OPPOSITE OF LIFE IS . . ?

1 There are many options to find a copy of Rumi's poem *The Guest House*. Coleman Barks is often recognised as the leading translator of his work into English.

2 George Best quotes can be found in many places on the Internet. He was known for his wit amongst many other things including being one of the world's greatest ever football players. Watching him play was joyful. Hearing him speak, alongside footballer Rodney Marsh, was entertaining, just like his football.

3 Patrick Kavanagh was an Irish poet and novelist. His best-known works are the poems *On Raglan Road* and *The Great Hunger*. His best-known novel is *Tarry Flynn*. His accounts of the everyday and commonplace in Irish life made his writing bristle with aliveness.

4 The Circle of Hearts Medicine Wheel in Milton Keynes took up nine months of my life helping to guide it into the world. It is worth a visit, and to see the area around Willen Lake that includes The Peace Pagoda, Temple, Labyrinth, Tree Cathedral and the lakes. If you are sensitive to earth energies, you will love this place.

5 Stony Stratford is a beautiful market town and 'coaching stop' that is now part of the city of Milton Keynes. It is worth a visit too, to check out The Cock and The Bull and other historic buildings. You can read more about it here: *https://www.stonystratford.co.uk/*

6 *The Yoga Sutras of Patanjali* translated and introduced by Alistair Shearer is an easy to read, easy to digest version of these infinite and great principles. ISBN 978-1-84-604283-6.

7 Andy Thomas is a leading researcher, writer and speaker on all forms of mysterious and hidden phenomena. He is also the organiser of The Glastonbury Symposium held each year in July in Glastonbury. You can find out more at *https://truthagenda.org/* and *https://glastonburysymposium.co.uk/*. A great festival, I highly recommend it.

8 *Strange* by Andy Thomas is a comprehensive investigative book that covers the so-called paranormal incidents that many of us have experienced in one way or another. It is a great read, and I can vouch for The Hopi Rain Dance incident. ISBN 978-1-78678-837-2.

9 Kath Temple is a leading teacher on happiness and well-being. Kath is one of the world's most brilliant therapeutic practitioners. You can check out her work at The Life Long Learning Company: *https://lifelonglearningcompany.com/* and The Happiness Foundation: *https://thehappinessfoundation.co.uk/team/kath-2/*.

10 Extreme Ironing is dangerous. For best results, iron safely at home, but watch out for flying rings if you iron overseas. *https://coolofthewild.com/extreme-ironing/*

11 *The Sixth Sense* starring Bruce Willis and is a 1999 psychological thriller with a great ending. Oh lord of the rings.

12. Ziba, In Hitchin, Hertfordshire, is a wonderful place to have a coffee, some Turkish food and listen to cool music of a very high quality on a Friday evening or Sunday afternoon.

13 Beetlejuice starring Michael Keaton, Alec Baldwin, Geena Davis, Catherine O'Hara, Winona Ryder and Jeffrey Jones, was a 1988 Tim Burton gothic horror comedy. Beetlejuice was a sleazy, mischievous and dangerous 'bio-exorcist'.

14 Marianne Williamson is a tour de force. She is a writer, speaker, minister and former candidate for President of The United States of America. Marianne has committed her life to peace and love and the understanding of who we really are beyond ideas of right and wrong doing, and thoughts and feelings of fear or inadequacy.

15 Brian Swimme is much more than a cosmologist or an author. e is a poet and a luminary, and an entertaining orator. Do check out his work, it is brilliant.

16 *The Hidden Heart of The Cosmos* by Brian Swimme, is a brilliant read. It explains beautifully the findings of Quantum Field science and cosmogenesis. ISBN 1-57075-281-8.

CHAPTER 7 - SET SAIL FOR THE SHORES OF YOUR HEART

1 *The Strange Case of Dr Jekyll and Mr Hyde* is a Gothic horror story written by Robert Louis Stevenson in 1886. Dr Jekyll becomes Mr Hyde due a laboratory experiment that goes badly wrong. With an understanding of how our personality/ego works and the desire for something more genuine, we can begin to say goodbye to Mr or Ms Hyde and free Dr Jekyll from his split personality transformations.

2 A dying Captain Miller tells Private Ryan to earn his second

chance of life, which proves to be his driving force for the rest of his life, as played out in the 1998 movie, Saving Private Ryan.

3 Khufu's solar barque from ancient Egypt is housed in the Grand Museum at Giza. It is estimated to be around two thousand five hundred years old. Worth a visit if ever you go to Giza to see the Great Pyramids.

4 Big *Dick and The Extenders* were a legend. As Big Dick, Jack Snipes entertained many a tourist and local alike with his fearless comedy and raucous act. It was hilarious to witness, although perhaps not so much, if you became a part of his routine. You can read about him here: *https://theconchtelegraph.com/issues/2015/december/page8-9.pdf*

5 John Alexander West was an archaeologist and 'revolutionary' writer on Egyptian history. He was also a wonderful and charismatic human being. His book Serpent in the Sky. The High Wisdom of Egypt, ISBN 9780835606912, is ground-breaking, with his evidence of water-erosion at The Sphinx fascinating, as was everything he taught and lectured on. It was a joy and an honour to spend time in Egypt with John. RIP John Alexander West.

6 Universal Studios Florida is a theme park located in Orlando that opened in 1990. Its rides are mostly based around TV and movie themes. Since I visited, other theme parks have been added to the Florida complex.

7 Disney World Orlando opened in 1971 as an entertainment resort complex, but was started in the nineteen sixties by Walt and his brother Roy to compliment Disneyland, which opened in Anaheim California in 1955.

8 *Blackbeard's Ghost* was a 1968 movie starring Peter Ustinov, Dean Jones and Suzanne Pleshette produced by Walt Disney Productions

9 *Shift Happens* by Robert Holden was published on September 21st 2000 by Hodders, is now available from Hay House ISBN 9781401931704

10 *Anthem* is a song written by Leonard Cohen from the album *The Future* and released in 1992.

11 *The Voyage* is a song written by Irish singer and songwriter Johnny Duhan, which made famous by Christy Moore's release in 1989. Duhan went on to a record a version himself, released on his album of the same name in 2005.

12 *Into the Mystic* is a 1970 song by Van Morrison that featured on his *Moondance* album.

13 *The Calling* is a song written and performed by Shawn Gallaway from the album *'I Choose Love'* released in 2003. You can buy the album by using this link: *https://music.apple.com/us/album/i-choose-love/5082923* or by finding him at Apple Music or searching for him on YouTube.

EPILOGUE

1 The tale of two wolves is believed to be a Cherokee legend and is usually framed as a Grandfather speaking to his young grandson. The old wise man tells of a battle between two wolves that live inside the heads of all people. One is a wolf of fear, judgment and anger and the other wolf one of love, peace and unity. The young grandson is fascinated and asks his Grandfather which one will win. The Grandfather, takes a deep breath and replies: "The one that you feed."

2 *Pretty Vacant* is a song written and performed by *The Sex Pistols*, which was released in the UK on 1st July 1977. It obtained notoriety partly due to the way John Lydon sang the word vacant, in a time when the rebellious nature of punk rock was mirroring some of the Anarchy in the UK, which had been The Sex Pistols first release in November 1976.

Printed in Dunstable, United Kingdom